Lessons from Genesis:

A Study Companion
Volume 1

Dennis McCallum

Copyright 2020 by Dennis McCallum

International Standard Book Number:
978-0-9976057-7-8

NEW PARADIGM
Publishing

Contents:

Introduction

Genesis is a story; a true story. In this book, we follow that story, analyzing what it means for us. This isn't a commentary. It's accessible to any reading believer, including newer Christians. As you go through Genesis in your personal study, or read with a friend, this book can help answer the questions that come up. It focuses on the main message of the text. At the same time, we address some of the key critical issues, mainly in the footnotes.

This book also defends the Genesis text. Genesis has been under intense attack for the past three hundred years, reaching a crescendo in our own day. Source division, genre criticism, and literary analysis all seem to lead to the same conclusion: Genesis is not literal history. Its statements are false.

We will approach the text with a high view of scripture—a view that comes directly from Jesus. He regularly quoted and referred to this book as scripture. He also said "the scripture cannot be broken" (John 10:35). And when quoting Genesis, he said, "God said..." (Matthew 19:4-5). To those who adopt such a high view of scripture, the final author of Genesis and all biblical books is God. That means that we should harmonize what we find in Genesis with what we find elsewhere in scripture.

Secular scientist often joins the chorus of critics. But in addition to actual scientific findings, another voice emerges—scientism—a faith-based ideology that insists on natural cause and effect as the necessary explanation to all things. It also holds that no real knowledge is possible apart from empirically verified scientific findings.

We will show that this approach (also known as methodological naturalism) is unproven and fails to explain our world. It is, in fact, a false faith position that should be rejected. It also is self-refuting, because it fails its own test, being a philosophical claim, not a scientific finding.

Finally, at every point, we will try to understand how the spiritual principles illustrated in Genesis apply to our personal spiritual growth and ministries.

1 The Importance of Genesis

Bible-believing Christians believe that every book in the canon of scripture is inspired by God, so the books are alike in that regard. However, not all books are the same in importance. We could lose some books without losing the truths they contain, because those truths are contained in other books as well.

Not so with Genesis. Genesis is in the first rank of important books in scripture. This book is full of information that is not found in any other book of the Bible.

In fact, Genesis is the base or stand upon which the rest of the Bible rests. Without that base, much of the rest of the Bible would be unintelligible.

Think of some of the key truths Genesis brings to us:

- The story of creation
- The critical concept of humans created in God's image
- Humanity's fall from God's will
- The introduction of humans' fallen nature
- The chaos, bloodshed, and evil that spread to the ancient world
- God's selection of Abraham, and the launching of his plan of rescue for the human race.
- How God protected and advanced his plan through his ancient people for the next two hundred years.
- The set up for the next book, Exodus. Who are the children of Israel, and why are they in Egypt?

Where would we be without these crucial truths that underlie the whole Bible? Confused!

Authorship

Unlike the other books in the Pentateuch, Genesis contains no claim that Moses wrote it.[1] Yet, conservative scholars believe he did. Ancient Jews also believed he did. In fact, we have several good reasons to believe in Mosaic authorship.

The Pentateuch as a unit

The Old and New testaments group the first five books in the Bible together under titles like "the law, or teaching, (Heb. *torah*) of Moses" (Joshua 1:7), "the book of the law" (Joshua 24:26), or "the book of the law of the Lord" (2 Chronicles 17:9). They envision Moses as the author of a single five book collection—the "Pentateuch."

Notice Jesus' three-fold grouping of Old Testament scripture: "Everything written about me in 1) the law of Moses, 2) the prophets, and 3) the psalms, must be fulfilled" (Luke 24:44). Which group would Genesis fit in? The Psalms? No. The prophets? No. Clearly, he was referring to the Pentateuch, and, he was saying that as part of the Pentateuch, Genesis is one of Moses' books.

Jesus also has Abraham, in the parable of Lazarus and the rich man, saying "They have Moses and the Prophets; let them hear them" (Luke 11:29). This was the typical way rabbis referred to the whole Old Testament. By using the same expression when telling the parable, Jesus showed that he too knew Moses wrote the whole Pentateuch.[2]

You can also see the Jews' view in Jesus' day because ancient Jewish scholars like Josephus and Philo both attribute Genesis' authorship to Moses.[3]

Other rabbis referred to being "circumcised according to the custom of Moses" (Acts 15:1). Only Genesis 17 explains

---

[1] Other books in the Pentateuch do claim Mosaic authorship. See Exodus 17:14; 24:4; 33:1-2; 34:27; Deuteronomy 31:9, 11; Numbers 21:9.

[2] Other examples of references to Mosaic authorship include Matthew 19:8; Mark 12:26; John 5:46-47; 7:19; Acts 3:22; Romans 10:5.

[3] Josephus, *Antiquities* IV 8.48, and Philo, *Life of Moses* 3:39.

circumcision, not the rest of the Pentateuch. So they were saying that Moses wrote Genesis.

Naturalistic attacks

No one should ever take seriously the gratuitous attacks on Mosaic authorship launched by liberal, naturalistic theologians during the past three centuries. According to these theories, Genesis is folklore from the first millennium BC (i.e., 800 to 600 BC), not from the second millennium (1400's BC), when Moses really lived. They usually deny that such a person as Moses ever even existed.[4] They deny that the Jews were ever in Egypt or that an Exodus occurred.[5]

These skeptical scholars think the stories in Genesis are fables, some from northern Israel and some from southern Israel, at the time called Judah. Next, a later redactor clumsily stitched them together a thousand years after Moses' time, hoping to unify the different mythologies. As a result, they claim that a careful reader can discern at least four different sources, known as J, E, D, and P in the Pentateuch. This segmenting into different sources is called the "documentary hypothesis."

The JEDP scenario and related schemes have all been ably and decisively refuted for anyone open-minded enough to

---

[4] Bruggeman is typical in his comments about Joseph's account in Genesis: "It is commonly agreed that the Joseph narrative is a work of art designed to make a statement to Israel. For such expression, questions of historicity are inappropriate." So fictional stories like these have nothing to do with history. That's far from what Jesus said when stating plainly that these accounts were historical (e.g. John 8:56). So if you start out denying the historicity of Genesis, you end up denying the truthfulness of Jesus. Walter Bruggeman, *Genesis: Interpretation: A Bible Commentary for Teaching and Preaching* (Louisville, KY: Westminster John Knox Press, 2010) 290.

[5] Naturalistic scholarship denies the Jewish people were ever in Egypt and yet the Brooklyn Papyrus lists the names of a number of slaves and the list includes nine Hebrew names! Another find in the Tomb of Rekmire shows Hebrew slaves making bricks from mud and straw. Both finds fall within the time when the Hebrew enslavement fell. Titus Kennedy, *Unearthing the Bible: 101 Archaeological Discoveries that Bring the Bible to Life*, (Eugene, OR: Harvest House2020) 48-51. Neither of these or other finds were available when liberal scholars formed their theories.

read. The fact that this foolish scheme is still taught as fact in secular universities is pathetic. British scholar K. A. Kitchen excoriates current Old Testament liberal scholars, observing, "The role of theory is preponderant." Specifically,

> Nowhere else in the whole of Ancient Near Eastern history has the literary, religious and historical development of a nation been subjected to such drastic and wholesale reconstructions at such variance with the existing documentary evidence.[6]

This is a critical point. In the 1700s and 1800s deistic, enlightenment scholars divided the Pentateuch into multiple "sources." These sources were not based on any documentary evidence. They were imagined based on speculation about the one, single source—the Old Testament. Kitchen, an Egyptologist and secular archeologist, marvels that liberal, unbelieving Biblical scholars are all alone when they dissect an ancient text this way.

Source division was driven, not by textual discovery or by archeology, but by philosophical assumptions such as religious Darwinism.[7] They impose such theories on the text, while ignoring the many valid parallels emerging in ancient Near Eastern studies that affirm the Bible's historical claims.

Kitchen points out that, regrettably, "Old Testament scholarship has made only superficial use of Ancient Near Eastern data." One of the main causes of the documentary hypothesis is, according to Kitchen, ignorance. Archeology

---

[6] K. A. Kitchen, *The Ancient Orient and Old Testament* (Wheaton: Intervarsity Press, 1975) 20. He adds, "Even the most ardent advocate of the documentary theory must admit that we have as yet *no single scrap* of external, objective *(i.e., tangible)* evidence for either the existence or the history of 'J', 'E', or any other alleged source-document. 23.

[7] Religious Darwinism assumes that religion in any given area evolves from primitive animism, to polytheism, to henotheism (the view that the local, national god is bigger and stronger than other gods), to a more transcendent view of God such as theism or pantheism. Higher critics think they see these stages by reading between the lines in the Pentateuch.

was one of the later fields of science to develop. That's why scholars like Karl Graff and Julius Wellhausen (key originators of JEDP) had no access to our greatest finds. These include tens of thousands of near eastern tablets that bear directly on the Old Testament—all discovered after their time.

These are the findings Kitchen has in mind when he says, "The comparative material from the Ancient Near East is tending to agree with the extant structure of Old Testament documents as actually transmitted to us, rather than with the reconstructions of nineteenth-century Old Testament scholarship."[8]

He documents scores of examples where our findings from the second millennium fit Old Testament usage, but do not fit first millennium usage (which is when liberal higher critics claim these books were written).

He also demonstrates how liberal Old Testament scholars seem to remain unaware of these findings, as they continue to drive their outdated, theory-laden views. This has been the case from the beginning of the development of the documentary hypothesis.

Gleason Archer's historical coverage of the tortured, constantly shifting stages this view went through is hilarious, if not for the tragic fact that thousands of a people have had their faith shredded by theories with no factual backing.[9]

Internal evidence

Careful reading of Genesis leads to the conclusion that this book has features unmistakably pointing to Mosaic authorship in the 1400 BC time period. It also exhibits the

---

[8] Kitchen, *Ancient Orient*, 25.

[9] Gleason Archer, *Survey of Old Testament Introduction*, (Chicago: Moody, 2007) 66-80. Most people are unaware that this theory went through dozens of generations, all contradicting each other, before more or less solidifying as the JEDP theory.

perspective of people raised in Egypt rather than in Canaan. Of course, according to Genesis, Jews in Moses' day had never been in Canaan. They had lived in Egypt for hundreds of years.

For example, consider Genesis 13:10:

> Lot looked up and saw that the whole plain of the Jordan was well watered, like the garden of the Lord, like the land of Egypt, toward Zoar. (NIV)

Anyone who has been to Israel knows that the Jordan valley is the predominant geographical feature in this small country. It's an enormous rift valley with mountain ranges on either side, running the length of the country. Nobody who lived in this country could fail to know about this valley and the river Jordan running down the center.

How odd, then, that the author feels the need to explain that the valley is well watered, and then goes on to elaborate that it's similar to the land of Egypt as you go toward Zoar! Clearly, the author and audience are not from Israel, but from Egypt. Yet this fact is nowhere accepted by liberal theories.

Moses and the Jewish nation had been in Egypt until their release described in the book of Exodus. Moses may have visited Canaan during the forty years he was a shepherd around Midian, because nomadic shepherds sometimes wander far and wide. But the rest of the people were slaves in Egypt, and none of them would know anything about Israel, except what Moses told them. This passage perfectly fits the historical scenario given in the Pentateuch, but flies directly in the face of liberal theories.

According to liberal scholars, the whole story about Egypt was mythology, and there was no such person as Moses. They claim these folk stories originated in Canaan among people who never lived anywhere else.

Think about this. If this account is phony and actually originates from hundreds of years after a supposed exodus from Egypt, why would the author frame it this way? Are we to seriously think that an 800 BC author would fudge the account, inserting verses like these so later, modern critics would think it was from 1400 and written to native Egyptians? That's so absurd! Are we to think that this spurious author saw the need to explain to resident Israelites what the Jordan valley is like—and then use an area in Egypt to help them understand?

The most reasonable way to make sense of this verse is to accept that the author and audience share a knowledge of Egypt, but not of the land of Canaan. No time or group in the 800s fits that scenario.

Other examples detailed by Archer:

- Only an eye witness would include details like those in Exodus 15:27 where the narrator recalls the exact number of fountains (twelve) and of palm trees (seventy) at Elim, in the desert. Why would a later imposter include that?

- The author of the Pentateuch demonstrates a thorough acquaintance with Egypt including multiple proper names and place names (e.g., Gen 41:45). Remember, people in ancient times didn't take vacations in other countries. Travel was highly restricted.

- The Pentateuch has more Egyptian words than other Old Testament books.

- The seasons and weather referred to in the narrative are Egyptian, not Canaanite.

- The flora and fauna referred to are Egyptian or Sinaitic, never distinctively Palestinian.

- Genesis 23:2 refers to the well-known city, Hebron, and explains that it's a city in Canaan. Numbers 13:22 adds the detail that "Now Hebron was built seven years before Zoan in Egypt." Again, the author and readers must know more about Egypt than

Canaan. Genesis 33:18 does the same thing: "Shechem, which is in the land of Canaan."

- Numbers 2:1-31 explains the encampment and the exact location of the twelve tribes on the four sides of the tabernacle—perfectly appropriate to the generation of Moses, but with no relevance to any later generation. Yet liberals think this text was written after the Jews had lived in Canaan for almost a thousand years. So too with the exact order of march, recounting how each tribe and clan broke camp, in Numbers 10:14-20.

- Based on finds at Ebla, Ras Shamra, Nuzi, and Tel Amarna (all excavations from the second and third millennia BC), scholars have found that Genesis often refers to archaic customs from the second millennium BC. But these same customs had vanished before the first millennium (when liberals say it was written). How would spurious authors know this detailed history and culture from a thousand years before their time?[10]

We conclude that Moses was the author of Genesis, writing at the time of the Exodus.

The date of writing

Based on the previous finding, that Moses is the author, the time frame is clearly second millennium BC. However, this doesn't settle the question of dating the book, because conservative scholars, hold to two distinct scenarios, or chronologies, for the life of Moses.

The early chronology has Moses living in the fifteenth century and the Exodus in 1440 BC. The late chronology has Moses living in the thirteenth century and the exodus in approximately 1285 BC.

---

[10] These are a few examples of the many he covers with full documentation. Gleason Archer, *Introduction*, 115-121.

I am not going to cover this debate in detail here, because this not an academic book. But I will briefly explain why I believe the early chronology is correct.

1 Kings 6:1 says in part, "…in the four hundred and eightieth year after the sons of Israel came out of the land of Egypt," Solomon began to build the temple. Because of correlations with other ancient accounts and astronomical events like comets and eclipses, Bible-believing historians widely agree on dates for Old Testament events from the time of King Saul onward. Sources offering different dates do so only because they reject the truthfulness of biblical chronological statements.

The date for the beginning of the temple is 960 BC within one or two years. Add to this add the four hundred and eighty years mentioned, and we arrive at 1440 BC. That's the early chronology's date for the Exodus. Arrival in the land of Canaan would be forty years later in 1400 BC. Genesis was probably written during those forty years, as argued above.

This date also fits another chronological claim. In Judges 11:26, Jephthah states that the Israelites had possession of the land for some 300 years. This again points to a time around 1400 BC.

The late chronology

Those holding the late chronology argue that the early view can't be correct because Genesis 47:11 and Exodus 1:11 refer to Pharaoh Ramses during the time of Israel's sojourn in Egypt. Ramses I reigned until 1290 BC—long after the 1440 date.

The late chronology attempts to fit the exodus and the conquest of Canaan into the interval between the death of Ramses (Exodus 2:23) and the Mernephta Stele, a stone obelisk with engravings, reliably dated to 1208 BC. The Stele refers by name to an Egyptian attack on Israel showing that the nation of Israel was already in the land.

This is a very tight fit, and really doesn't work. It's missing the added forty years when Moses was exiled before the exodus. It also allows little time for the conquest.

It's much easier to see the references to Ramses as updates to the name added by a later copyist. Such modernizations are not unusual. For instance, Genesis 35:6 says, "So Jacob came to Luz (that is, Bethel), which is in the land of Canaan...." Or, Genesis 13:18 says Mamre is linked to Hebron. This would be like someone writing about early frontier events in my area and calling it "Ohio" instead of "the land of the Mohicans," even though it wasn't a state yet.

Other elements of the debate have to do with archeology, with both sides offering pros and cons. It's too detailed to cover here. Both sides put up plausible scenarios, at the same time they change their arguments from time to time— for instance, changing the best date for various layers in excavated cities.

In the end, the full burden of evidence falls on those who reject the testimony of the original sources. Even though they try to explain 1 Kings 6 being off by including overlapping periods, their late chronology argument isn't persuasive.

We conclude that Moses wrote Genesis between 1440 and 1400 BC.[11]

Other sources?

Even if we accept Mosaic authorship, how do we explain him knowing about things that happened long before he lived? Genesis goes all the way back to creation in its coverage. Most Bible believing scholars argue that Moses had access to oral or written sources that he combined under the guidance of the Holy Spirit. The effort to pick out these "memoranda" is what got Jean Astruc—the original

---

[11] For a more detailed defense of the late chronology, see James K. Hoffmeier, "What is the biblical date for the Exodus?" *JETS,* Vol. 50 #2 (June 2007) 225–47.

source divider—started on the Documentary Hypothesis in 1753.

I think the idea that written or oral records could have survived from the time of Abraham, let alone from creation, is much harder to believe than the idea that God told Moses directly what to write. He was on the mountain with God for a long time—way longer than it would take to write the sections in Exodus that were obviously written on the mountain (like the dictated ten commandments). Even after his time on the mountain, Moses regularly went into the tabernacle to talk to God. We don't know what they were talking about.

We know God sometimes dictated things to Moses with the words, "Write this down on a scroll as a permanent reminder…" (Exodus 17:14, also 34:27). So why wouldn't God also tell him the story of humanity and have him write that?

Exodus never mentions any written or oral record that Moses might have used. Godly Jews had probably kept stories of their ancestors alive, but not in a condition suitable to inspired scripture. Our accounts in Genesis from the earliest times are detailed, including, for instance, word for word dialogs.

Instead of retaining an accurate history, it seems like the whole nation had grown rather distant from God during their time in slavery. Idol worship was common (Amos 5:26-27). Unbelief was evident both before and after their departure from Egypt. So it's unlikely they had the discipline or the interest to keep an accurate history over hundreds of years.

To suppose that this group would help to explain Moses' knowledge of primordial history, or even the patriarchs, is quite implausible. What would keep these written or oral tales infallible? Or if, as some claim, God directed him which parts of the earlier accounts to accept or reject, Is that any different than him just telling Moses the stories?

While it's possible that some records or oral stories of some kind existed, it's more likely that God simply told, or showed Moses what happened and then later, his Holy Spirit aided Moses' recollection as he wrote it.

The big picture

The Jews of antiquity and the early church always accepted that Moses wrote Genesis under the inspiration and direction of God in the fifteenth century BC. Nothing discovered since then gives us any reason to think otherwise.

Moses was highly qualified to author the opening books of the Bible. He lived at a time when the first phonetic alphabet appeared using representation of phonemes by the letters of the alphabet—the so-called phonetic alphabet (like our writing today). The invention of the alphabet happened in Canaan at about 1500 BC.[12] Our earliest sample comes from a turquoise mine in the Sinai—near where Moses herded.[13]

He was prepared for his mission for decades, including a royal education in the most advanced culture of his day—Egypt. Finally, called and claimed by God, he spent forty years guiding the people of Israel through the wilderness—that's plenty of time to write the Pentateuch or even far more than that. God had his man, and the time was right to set down in writing the story of beginnings.

---

[12] "The first so-called Proto-Sinaitic or Proto-Canaanite alphabet, which originated in the region of present-day Lebanon, took advantage of the fact that the sounds of any language are few. It consisted of a set of 22 letters, each standing for a single sound or voice, which, combined in countless ways, allowed for an unprecedented flexibility for transcribing speech." Denise Schmandt-Besserat, "The Evolution of Writing," https://sites.utexas.edu/dsb/.

[13] David Porush, "The Origin of the Alphabet: Part 1," (DavidPoresh.com) 2015.

2 Genesis 1: Creation

Genesis 1:1

> In the beginning, God created the heavens and the earth. (Genesis 1:1)

This grand claim leaps off the first line of the Bible, and undergirds everything thereafter. The language is constructed in a way that makes this a pure and total beginning of all things.

Before discussing different views on the origin and history of life on earth, we will consider the larger picture of the origin of the universe itself. We want to assess the atheistic/agnostic view and the theistic view.

Atheistic/agnostic cosmology

When I was an atheist in the sixties, we never saw the origin of the universe as a problem. It simply existed, and no doubt always had. Later, we gradually began hearing that the universe was expanding, but we accepted the idea that it was probably eternally oscillating in and out.

Only later did science teachers begin to admit the unthinkable from a naturalistic view: that the universe had an absolute beginning point around fourteen billion years ago. It was an embarrassment to naturalists, and maybe that's why it took so long to reach mainstream teaching.

The discovery happened all the way back in 1922 and 1927 respectively when Alexander Friedmann and Georges Lemaître inferred from Einstein's equations of general relativity, that the universe might be expanding, contrary to the so-called "static state" view. Eventually Edwin Hubble confirmed their theory in 1929 when he measured the "red shift" proving that all galaxies were moving away from each other.

It was Lemaître again in 1931 who put together the additional implication from the expansion of the universe, that if one projected the outward movement of the universe backward in time, it was smaller and smaller. Eventually, all the mass of the universe would have been concentrated at a single point. That meant that somehow, everything had to burst out from that point.

The term "big bang" didn't appear until 1949 when Fred Hoyle (who hated the idea) used the expression derisively on a radio show. But most people didn't know about it until the seventies, when it became common knowledge.

By then, I was a believer. I remember some Bible teachers denouncing the notion of the big bang as an invention of "heathen" scientists. I never understood that view. Isn't it exactly what theistic creation would predict?

Yes! Atheistic scientists saw this implication immediately. Arthur Eddington wrote in 1931, "the notion of a beginning is repugnant to me... I simply do not believe that the present order of things started off with a bang... the expanding Universe is preposterous... incredible... it leaves me cold."[1]

As recently as 1989, John Maddox, the atheistic editor for the journal, *Nature*, wrote an article entitled "Down with the Big Bang." In it he plainly admitted his view: "Apart from being philosophically unacceptable, the Big Bang is an over-simple view of how the Universe began, and it is unlikely to survive the decade ahead... It will be a surprise if it somehow survives the Hubble telescope."[2] His words ring hollow today, now that big-bang cosmology has become the universal consensus.

---

[1] Cited in Robert Jastrow, *God and the Astronomers,* (New York: Norton, 1978) 105.

[2] John Maddox, "Down with the Big Bang," *Nature,* 340 (10 August 1989): 425.

Consider what big bang cosmology claims: first there was nothing. Agnostic theoretical physicist Paul Davies explains,

> In the past [the universe] was smaller. If we run the expansion in reverse for 13.7 billion years, then the ball shrinks to a single point, a single, sizeless dot. And then…? Nothing—the ball has vanished! The nothing before the big bang really is "no thing"—neither matter nor space. Nothing.[3]

This is the standard view among physicists. Space and time form a continuum, and both appeared at the big bang. World famous atheistic scholar, Stephen Hawking said, "Almost everyone now believes that the universe, and time itself, had a beginning at the Big Bang."[4]

Davies summarizes,

> We are left with a puzzle. Why should a ball of matter suddenly appear out of nowhere, at some particular moment in time and at some particular location in preexisting empty space, when this event hasn't happened for all eternity up to that moment? What would cause it to happen, and happen just then and just there? There is no satisfactory answer.[5]

No kidding—unless you believe in God. To explain the big bang you need a cause that lies outside the universe (the universe can't cause itself). Such a cause must be outside time (because time began at the big bang). Anything that would cause the big bang must be timeless, non-material, probably extra dimensional, and extremely powerful. Do we know anyone like that?

Non-believers are in a difficult position these days. How would you like to defend the idea that there was nothing,

---

[3] Paul Davies, *Cosmic Jackpot: Why Our Universe Is Just Right for Life*, (NY: Houghton Mifflin Harcourt; 1 edition, 2007), 66.

[4] Stephen Hawking, "The Nature of Space and Time," *The Isaac Newton Institute Series of Lectures*, 2015.

[5] Paul Davies, *Cosmic Jackpot*, 66.

and then suddenly, for no known reason, there was everything? Big bang cosmology advances a picture of the origin of the universe that cries out for an explanation.

Interestingly, thousands of years ago, the Bible declared,

> By faith we understand that the entire universe was formed at God's command, that what we now see did not come from anything that can be seen. (Hebrews 11:3)

The idea of everything coming out of nothing for no reason is untenable. For one thing, that would destroy all science. Science is based on determining cause and effect. If the big bang can happen without cause, anything can happen.

As theists, we realize that something has always existed. The question is what? Matter and energy? No! We just saw that they came into existence at the big bang.

So what then? Isn't it far more likely that whatever is eternal is a spiritual, rather than a material, entity? As such, a spiritual being would not be subject to the laws of nature. The theistic view is much stronger than any non-theistic view for this reason.

More problems

Non-theists don't have an explanation for the big bang, as Davies admitted above. But their situation has worsened immensely during the past few decades.

In the early eighties, physicists began reporting at scientific conferences about something called "fine-tuning." These studies demonstrated that the physical forces in the universe (the strong and weak nuclear force, electromagnetic force, and gravity) as well as a number of other constants have a strength relative to each other that seems incredibly fortunate or "fine-tuned."

For instance, if the force of gravity was stronger or weaker than it currently is by one part in 10^{40} the universe would have collapsed back on itself long ago, or flown apart preventing life-giving star formation.

As scientists looked into it further, they began to realize that dozens of other variables were also finely tuned—even more so. For instance, the speed of the outward motion in the first fractions of a second after the big bang could not have been faster or slower by even one part in 10^{55}.

To understand this number, consider how many miles are in a light-year—about six trillion. But what about the number of inches? Much larger—3.7×10^{17} inches. But that's nowhere near ten to the fifty-fifth. If we go down to $1/10^{th}$ of an inch it doesn't change much. That only takes us up one order of magnitude to 10^{18}. How quickly will we reach $1/100^{th}$ of an inch? Really quick. It again only takes us to 10^{19} and by now we're at the width of a human hair compared to a light year.

We're looking for a number equal to 10^{55}. What about hitting a mark as wide as a human hair in ten light years? Again, that only moves us up one order of magnitude—10^{20}. To describe a number as large as we're talking about we would have to add more light years—trillions of them. We are now talking about a point the width of one human hair in a string 10^{35} light-years long!

We can't really imagine a number that large, but the confusion has only begun. We saw that the force of gravity finely tuned to one part in 10^{40} *and* the speed of the big bang has to be finely tuned to one part in 10^{55}. But it's not one or the other, it's *both*. Both variables have to be exactly that at the same time—like two long strings that cross each other at one place. And what are the chances of that? The chances are 10^{40} *times* 10^{55}! This is a truly unimaginable number, especially when we realize there are a couple dozen more fine tuned variables necessary for life of any kind to exist.

This puzzle has been a leading reason that a number of world class scientists and intellectuals have changed their minds from unbelief, to belief in God in recent years.

For instance, Francis Collins, a National Medal of Science winner, wrote a book called *The Language of God*, in which he recounts how he couldn't resist the logic of creation, mainly because of cosmological fine tuning.

He explains,

> The chance that all of these constants would take on the values necessary to result in a stable universe capable of sustaining complex life forms is almost infinitesimal. And yet those are exactly the parameters that we observe. In sum, our universe is wildly improbable.[6]

When I was a young Christian, the argument from design (that the world manifests design, and therefore a designer must exist) was more intuitive, but still strong—nothing like it is today. Findings in cosmology combine with findings in physics have created a stronger case than at any other time in history.

Multiverse?

Secular thinkers produced the multiverse theory to explain fine tuning. Under this theory, our universe is only one of many parallel worlds. Many, many parallel worlds! The theory ranges from trillions to infinite other universes.

You can see why. The numbers are so huge against the chances of fine-tuning that only an astronomical number of universes could be expected to come up with what we see. Problem solved.

Or is it?

Remember, we've never seen any of these universes; never measured anything about them; never will encounter them

---

[6] Francis Collins, *The Language of God: A Scientist Presents Evidence for Belief*, (NY: Free Press, 2007) 74.

in any way. Are we quite sure this wasn't made up? How could we ever know?

Most people are unaware of one instructive fact: When did the multiverse theory originate? According to the authoritative essay, "A brief history of the multiverse" by Andrei Linde, himself an early proponent, the year was 1982. That should bring a smile to the lips, because that was right when the early scientific papers on fine tuning were coming out. What are the odds? No sooner did we discover that the universe is astonishingly fine tuned, than we also discovered trillions of invisible universes!

Surely there was some discovery, some new observation, some math formula that explains the appearance of multiverse theory, right? No. Nothing can account for it but a desire to explain away fine-tuning.

And there's one more problem. Agnostic astrophysicist Paul Davies admits,

> Multiverse only moves the problem up from the universe to the multiverse. If other universes did exist, they, or the universe generating mechanism would require fine-tuning in their own right.[7]

Yes! Where did these trillions of other universes come from? Double talk like "bubble-universes" offer no explanation for anything. If the multiverse turned out to be true, we wouldn't be a single step closer to an explanation for what we see.

The multiverse theory is not science, but raw imagination. Worse, it's a refusal to consider the most plausible explanation for fine tuning no matter what the evidence shows.

---

[7] Paul Davies, *Cosmic Jackpot* He also says, "In the theory of eternal inflation we cannot directly observe the other pocket universes for two reasons: because they are unbelievably far away, and because they are receding from us much faster than light. It can be validly objected that a theory that rests on entities that are in principle unobservable cannot be described as scientific."

The big picture

Science is supposed to be a search for truth using a rigorous method and observation of the real world. If that's true, and if God exists, it's likely that science will discover God in the course of its search.

That's what's happening. As science succeeds in ascertaining what the universe is and where it came from, theists are not surprised to see the hand of God all over everything they discover. "In the beginning, God created the heavens and the earth."

3 Choose a Planet

Genesis 1:1

We now know much of the history of earth up to our day, including the dramatic events surrounding the coming and the work of Jesus. God, of course, knew all this before the earth existed (Ephesians 1:4). His plan of rescue for the human race affects not only us, but also the whole heavenly host of angels (Ephesians 3:10).

As part of this plan, he has a number in mind for how many people need to come to faith before he's done with history as we know it (Revelation 6:10). That means, considering how many people have come to faith since Jesus' time, he is looking for hundreds of millions or billions of followers before he ends this phase of history.

So, God needed a planet capable of sustaining high level life for a long time—no easy task. Notice that a planet that could conceivably sustain bacteria for a period of time isn't good enough. God's plan required much more.

Astronomers think the universe contains many billions of planets, including billions of earthlike planets. If that's true, we have no clear evidence of it. The claims are based on probability estimates. So far, about two thousand planets have been identified, and none of them are capable of sustaining advanced life.

Uniqueness of Earth

Perhaps other planets like Earth exist, but it wouldn't be easy to match the amazing suite of conditions here that work out to our advantage. For this section, I rely heavily on astrophysicist, Hugh Ross' excellent book, *Improbable Planet: How Earth Became Humanity's Home.*[1]

Nice star

First, our star is well suited to host a life-allowing planet. Most stars are part of double or group star systems.[2] That means a planet with a life-suitable orbit would be impossible for most stars.

The sun is also ideal in its size, age, and luminosity. It's very stable. It's nice too that it doesn't lie too close to our galaxy's center where the temperature would prohibit life.

Liquid water always available

Water is an amazing compound. It's by far the best solvent we know of. It has unique properties that come into play massively when it comes to life. Water is the medium in which metabolism and the other functions of the cell organelles happen. It's necessary at all levels of life.

Availability of large quantities of liquid water requires a balanced mix of suitable luminosity from the sun, distance from the sun, and atmospheric pressure.

It's important that water be liquid year round. Otherwise, if every part of the planet froze each year, it would have been very hard on the single-celled life that teamed in our early oceans. It would be like a annual reset that would greatly retard progress in evolution.

So far, planets discovered with water and carbon have too much of each. Relative to the average for planets its size, Earth has 1200 times less carbon based gasses, and 500 times less water. This allows continents to form. The thinness of Earth's atmosphere allows the development of

---

[1] Hugh Ross, *Improbable Planet: How Earth Became Humanity's Home,* (Grand Rapids: Baker Books, 2016).

[2] "Some studies suggest as many as 85 percent... belong to double or multiple star systems." Astronomy.com, Phil Harrington, "Fun with double and variable stars," December 4, 2006.

lungs. Both of these facts worked out well for high order life.

Awesome huge moon

Our moon is about fifty times larger than any other moon in the solar system relative to the mass of its host planet. That's incredibly large. Joseph Spradley explains some of the important contributions the moon has made favoring life on Earth:

1. The glancing collision that formed the Moon appears to have given Earth its initial five-hour rotation rate, much faster than any other planet in the solar system. As a result, the slowing action of the Moon and the Sun to our current rate of twenty four hours, spanned billions of years, allowing the development of conditions favorable to life.

2. The Moon-forming event—a collision by a Mars-sized asteroid—drove off much of Earth's atmosphere. That led to Earth avoiding an atmosphere like Venus (nearest to us in mass) where the atmospheric pressure is about 90 times ours. With too much carbon dioxide, the greenhouse effect leads to unlivable temperatures (average temperature of 864 degrees Fahrenheit). Our planet wouldn't be that hot, but the temperature on the hot side would certainly be much higher than the boiling point of water if our atmosphere was that thick.

3. The giant impact increased Earth's magnetic field to about 100 times larger than any other rocky planet. That strong field is critical to abundant life as we'll see.

4. The mass collision added to Earth's internal heat, aiding continental plate tectonics (unknown on any other planet). Tectonics recycle nutrients and keep carbon dioxide in balance through the carbon cycle.

5. The large size of our Moon produces sufficient gravitational force to keep the axis of Earth inclined in a narrow range between 22° and 25°, stabilizing annual climate variations in a favorable range for living organisms.[3]

Correct amount and type of ultraviolet light

Ultraviolet light catalyzes (speeds up) many organic chemical reactions essential for life. But too much ultra violet destroys terrestrial life and breaks down essential molecules. Earth is right where we need it to be.

This is especially handy for us because, with stars older than the sun (after the hydrogen burning phase has ended), the UV-habitable zone moves out far beyond the liquid water zone. That means the UV and liquid water zone won't overlap like they do on Earth. Astronomers estimate that 75% of the stars in the Milky Way are older than our sun.

Nice ozone layer

"Ozone in Earth's stratosphere absorbs 97-99 percent of the Sun's short wavelength, life-damaging UV radiation while allowing much of the longer wavelength, beneficial radiation to pass through."[4]

For a planet to develop an ozone shield, a number of factors have to be in balance: the right distance from its star, the right size and luminosity of the star. Stars larger or smaller than the sun emit widely variable levels of UV light which are not good for developing this shield.

Nice tilt

The earth has a 23 degree tilt on its axis. That's why we have seasons. If we didn't have that tilt, only narrow regions would be within a life-permitting temperature

---

[3]Joseph L. Spradley, "Ten Lunar Legacies: Importance of the Moon for Life on Earth," *Perspectives on Science and Christian Faith*, Vol. 62, Num. 4, Dec. 2010.

[4] Hugh Ross, *Improbable Planet*, 87.

range. The planet would have huge polar regions and small temperate regions. The earth's tilt warms the oceans and cools the continents. It produces the weather that circulates nutrients through erosion.

Nice size

Another "just-right" aspect of Earth is its size: If it was much smaller, it wouldn't have enough gravity to hold on to our precious atmosphere, but if it were much larger it might be a gas giant too hot for life.

Not tidally locked

The moon is tidally locked to the earth. That means the same side always faces the earth. Planets also become tidally locked to their stars if their orbits are too close. Mercury and Venus, for instance, are almost completely tidally locked.

If the earth were locked, one side would be frozen and the other side a furnace. All water would end up on the frozen side after boiling off on the hot side and being transmitted into the atmosphere. Crops would not be possible. Any habitable zone would be the tiny area between hot and cold, probably supporting nothing more than microorganisms.

Photosynthesis possible

Photosynthesis harvests energy from the sun and releases oxygen from carbon dioxide in the atmosphere. Photosynthetic bacteria and later plants converted Earth's atmosphere from being fatal for respiring creatures to becoming rich in free oxygen. But for photosynthesis to be possible, several variables need to be just so:

1. Light intensity from the star has to be within relatively narrow bounds
2. Ambient temperature has to be within a narrow range
3. Carbon dioxide concentration must be adequate

4. Mineral availability needs to be such that plants and other organisms can construct themselves
5. Liquid water quantity must be adequate

These conditions have to all overlap, which is unlikely. But our earth enjoys this and a host of other unlikely coincidences.

Protective magnetic field

Earth has a rare, powerful magnetic field that protects us from solar radiation, solar particles, and cosmic radiation. Without this field, these streams of radiation would wreak havoc on all life on earth.

Mars lacks such a field, and as a result, its atmosphere has been gradually driven off the planet by solar bombardment.

Earth is blessed with this field because of its iron core. Scientists have determined that to have a field like this,

1. The planet must have a liquid iron outer core

2. surrounding a solid iron inner core

3. with highly specific viscosity[5]

Protection from a big brother

Jupiter is an immense gas giant that acts like a vacuum cleaner, scooping up asteroids and comets that could annihilate life on earth.

The big picture

This is only a partial list of the needed features for any planet capable of maintaining high-order life. Did God select this planet because it was so unique? He apparently had many to choose from.

Or did he select a planet and modify it to be suitable for life? For example, something big struck the earth resulting

---

5 Hugh Ross, *Improbable Planet*, 91-92. He explains that a Japanese team showed that the planet's mass must fall within the range of 1.0-1.4 times the mass of Earth in order to have such a field last for billions of years.

in the formation of the moon. That event probably also gave us our tilted axis and magnetic field. Such an event would be exceedingly rare.

Atheistic scientists are eager to see billions of earth-like planets in order to provide very many opportunities for the most improbable event—the formation of life from non-living chemicals. So they have a motive for exaggerating.

Are there other habitable planets? Possibly. But the idea that they are common seems very unlikely when you study all of the specifics that make high-order life possible. Some scientists think Earth is very unusual and maybe even unique.

4 Life Arrives

Not long after the earth formed and cooled enough to form oceans, life appeared. The earliest fossils discovered so far are 3.46 billion years old, but scientists believe the beginning was much earlier.[1] All life was single-celled for more than three or maybe even four billion years.

Why so long?

If we accept that God created life, why would he let the planet sit for so long with nothing but single-celled organisms?

First, there's no hurry. God is an infinite being, so he's in no rush to carry out his plans. We can't imagine that, coming from our temporal perspective, but it's a factor.

Secondly, the long wait was probably necessary. The atmosphere of early earth was nothing like it is today—free oxygen was very rare, toxic gasses like methane, carbon dioxide, and ammonia were abundant. Only after billions of years of photosynthesis and anaerobic chemosynthesis did microscopic life gradually change the atmosphere on earth.

Near the time of the Cambrian Explosion, free oxygen reached unprecedented levels. Immediately, more advanced creatures appeared, based on respiration instead of photo or chemosynthesis.

During the same period, sulfate-reducing bacteria transformed much of the [poisonous] soluble metal resources in the oceans and crust into insoluble concentrated metal ore deposits. Without this gradual

---

[1] "The earliest direct evidence of life on Earth are microfossils of microorganisms permineralized in 3.465-billion-year-old Australian Apex chert rocks." https://en.wikipedia.org/wiki/Earliest_known_life_forms. But they add, "Earth had life at least 3.77 billion years ago, possibly as early as 4.28 billion years."

transformation, oceans and soil would have been fatally poisonous to higher life forms.

> This great diversity and abundance [of various bacteria] established early in life's history drove the carbon, nitrogen, oxygen, and sulfur cycles to levels eventually sufficient for the entry of advanced life.[2]

Requirements for life

A living organism must be capable of

- *Self-propagation:* Without this, evolution cannot happen. Without propagation, any organism would eventually die, leaving nothing behind. But self-propagation is incredibly difficult, as we will see.

- *Feeding:* Living organisms need some way to take in nutrients.

- *Metabolizing food into energy:* The operations within a cell require energy, and it has to be directed to very specific spots and in specific ways that bring about the needed reactions. Living cells have tiny, intricate factories that produce energy and store it in specialized molecules that function like batteries.

- *The ability to fabricate key compounds:* Cells are made of proteins, fats, carbohydrates, and nucleotides; and these are mostly created within the cell. That requires massive amounts of information.

---

[2] Hugh Ross, *Improbable Planet,* 110.

To understand how information relates to life, consider a pile of cut stone as pictured here. Suppose we insert explosive charges under the pile, and then detonate them. The force of the blast would propel the stones up into the air,

and then, they would fall back to the ground in roughly this shape.

Or not. Even my nine-year-old grandson when he saw this illustration, immediately declared "That won't happen!"

Of course not. The Taj Mahal's design contains immense quantities of relevant, specific information. The builders had to place each stone in a precise position and with a specific finish, according to the architect's plan.

But what if we repeated the experiment a billion times? That would make no difference. The materials needed for the building are present, and the blast supplies ample energy to move the pieces. But what will channel the energy into the precise work of assembling the building? That's where information comes in.

Instead of the Taj Mahal,
this blast would give us
something similar to the
picture on the right. And we
can safely predict that if we
repeated it a billion times,
every event would look quite

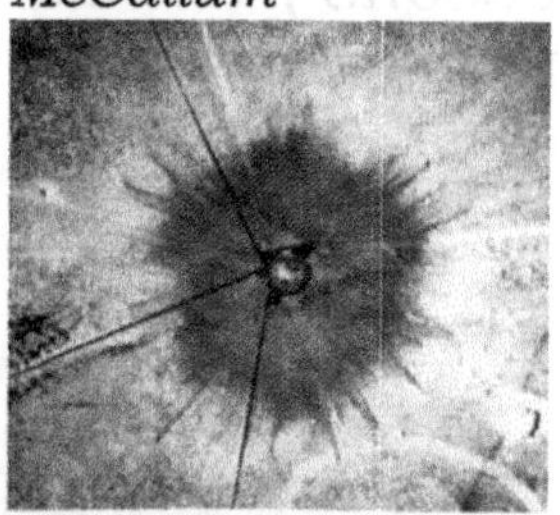

similar to this picture. This is what randomness looks like.

This is a key reason why the idea of living cells or even the
needed polymers spontaneously appearing from non-living
chemistry is implausible. Information is essential, but also
non-material. It can be recorded on a material medium, but
the information itself is not matter. So where does it come
from?

No evolution possible

Evolution definitely makes no contribution to abiogenesis
(the original transition from non-living molecules to living
organisms). Natural selection only operates *after* organisms
are reproducing. That's when random mutations in DNA
have a chance to make an organism more suitable for
survival in a given environment.

By definition, abiogenesis had to happen *before* any living
system capable of self-replication existed. Self-replicating
cells also have to be capable of metabolizing food and
adding newly created molecules (growth). The gap between
life and non-life is so vast that it screams for intelligent
design. Let's see why.

Thermodynamics

Some have suggested that natural forces of attraction,
might cause some of the needed compounds to form. But
this is now implausible. In fact, the opposite is the case.
Under natural conditions, especially those in a prebiotic
earth, the needed molecules of life don't form; they
disintegrate.

Professor of synthetic organic chemistry James Tour explains:

> Four types of molecules are needed for life: nucleotides, carbohydrates, proteins, and lipids. Origin of life researchers have spent a great deal of time trying to make these four classes of molecules, but with scant success. Claims that these structures could be prepared under prebiotic conditions… have never been realized.

Biologically significant polymers neither exist nor replicate themselves apart from already living organisms. One reason for this is that many of the reactions needed to form such molecules are either uphill thermodynamically or less favorable than countervailing reactions.

To understand this quandary, think about burning a piece of paper made from wood pulp. You need heat to get the reaction going, but once it's on fire, it continues to burn on its own. That's an exothermic reaction—giving off energy. It lets off energy, gasses, and reduces the paper to ash.

Now, what about capturing all the gasses released and all the ash, and reassembling them back into wood? That's not possible, because it would be endothermic—that is, "uphill," or unfavorable thermodynamically. This is how chemistry works.

However, a tree could take those chemicals and reassemble them into wood. Living organisms achieve this amazing ability to get around the laws of thermodynamics by using super-complex molecules called enzymes.

Enzymes

Enzymes are very large molecules often involving tens of thousands of atoms connected in very specific ways. They can use the energy from a favorable reaction to power, or drive, an unfavorable one.

All life uses these enzymes. They appear in the most ancient single celled life on earth, and that's not surprising, because assembling a living cell requires uphill reactions and enzymes make that possible. But enzymes are only produced by living organisms.

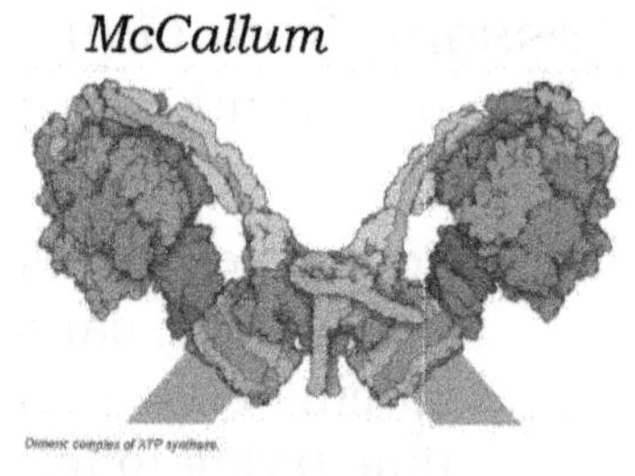

ATP Synthase has 75,614 atoms, all arranged precisely. This is one of the enzymes that create ATP, the battery molecules of the cell that are able to drive uphill reactions forward.

They never occur naturally apart from life. But in living cells, not just one or two, but thousands of enzymes work together in a perfectly coordinated fashion. And so, we have a cause and effect loop that requires something from outside itself. Having half the loop would be worthless. Only a creator could launch a system like this.

Cell membranes

Also, especially considering the harsh chemistry of the prebiotic earth, there's no way biologically significant polymers could form or last more than a very short time.

That's why living organisms have cell membranes (or cell *walls* for plants). The immense molecules involved in life are so fragile and vulnerable to unwanted counter-reactions that they have to be protected in a safe place. That safe place is the cell. Cells are surrounded by a membrane that only lets in desirable molecules. They also dispense with unwanted waste from inside the cell.

These membranes are amazingly complex, with millions of lipids (fats), proteins, and specialized carbohydrates. They never happen naturally apart from life. Yet, living organisms can't fabricate or preserve the molecules needed to build membranes without already having the protection of the membrane. So again, we have a causal loop with no beginning point. In the open ocean, even if polymers occasionally form, they break up or are altered long before they could actually be useful.

What about millions of years?

Isn't anything possible if you keep trying it long enough? In hundreds of millions of years, surely all needed compounds could form? No.

James Tour, an expert in synthetic organic chemistry, points out that when trying to generate one of the polymers useful to life, the chemist must seize the compound out of the reaction medium when it reaches usefulness and immediately separate it from the other reacting molecules. He must quickly put it in an inert setting, like a freezer. Otherwise, the same reaction that brought about the useful compound continues to caramelize it, and it becomes worthless.[3]

This is why time is not your friend when composing life-related polymers. Time, especially long periods of time, actually works against their formation or duration.

What about the RNA world?

Origin of life could not come about by natural means for another key reason: the ability to reproduce, even at the simplest level, requires multiple interdependent systems with elaborate codes in the cell.

DNA describes what is needed in a protein, but cannot produce it. Ribosomes can produce needed proteins, but have to get instructions from DNA via RNA. RNA can only temporarily contain the information and transfer it between DNA and ribosomes. The whole system has to be present (along with many other factors, including dazzlingly complex cascades of different enzymes) for the cell to grow and divide.

---

[3] James Tour, "Problems with abigenesis" https://www.youtube.com/watch?v=r4sP1E1Jd_Y. This short video is well worth watching. We can only cover a small part here.

To counter this problem, naturalistic scientists have suggested that, in place of this complex system found in modern cells, perhaps there was an earlier, simpler scenario, where RNA molecules simply duplicated themselves.

To be clear, RNA molecules do not replicate themselves today. They do catalyze, or drive, certain reactions, but those are far simpler than self-replication. Further, RNA is unstable and easily breaks down apart from the protection it gets in a cell. Then too, RNA is a very complicated molecule in its own right (roughly like DNA but containing only one side of the helix). Where do these complex RNA molecules come from? The theorists have no answer.

Finally, this scenario collides with our earlier discussion about information. To simply have a strand of RNA is really pointless, unless the arrangement of the bases corresponds to some needed protein. It's the difference between a blank sheet of paper and a sheet of paper with plans for the Taj Mahal drawn on it.

In a word, this whole picture of a world full of self-replicating RNA is imaginary; it never happens in the lab or in the real world and is unworthy of belief.

The big picture

In this chapter, we have seen multiple factors connected with the origin of life that are like arrows converging onto the same conclusion—God created life. Nothing can explain life other than a brilliant, all powerful creator. The closer we look at the origin of life, the more clear the conclusion becomes.

5 Six Days

Genesis 1:2-31

General observations

Genesis recounts creation in six days. We will explore different schools of interpretation for the days below. But first come some observations that are not linked to any school.

The order of creation is:

Day 1 (vs. 2-5)

a. Light.

b. The naming of light and darkness.

> Naming, to ancient Hebrew thinking, was exerting dominion over the person or thing named. Part of the message of the days of creation is that God reigns supreme over what he has made, and the naming demonstrates this. Compare this to Adam naming the animals in Chapter 2. In a day when people worshiped nature, this text shows that God made nature and owns it.

> At the end of each day, the expression appears, "And there was evening and there was morning, one day." This expression suggests these were real days, not ages. But those holding other views point out that the sun hadn't been created yet, so there wouldn't be a literal evening or morning.[1]

---

[1] Waltke thinks, "The lack of the definite article on each of the first five days suggests they may be dischronologized." Bruce Waltke, *Genesis* (Grand Rapids: Zondervan Academic) 62. Perhaps. But that is slim evidence. The days are still units of some kind of time. Also D. A. Sterchi, "Does Genesis 1 Provide a Chronological Sequence?" *JETS*, Vol. 39 (1996): 529-36.

God also "saw that the light was good," a refrain that appears over and over in this account (vs. 4, 10, 12, 18, 21, 25) Finally, at the end of the sixth day, "God saw all that He had made, and behold, it was very good." The refrain stands out against the subsequent story of the fall in Chapter 3. The statements declare that God created things well; it was humans who brought disaster.

Day 2 (vs. 6-8)

a. Creation of the "expanse" which is the atmosphere, dividing horizontally between land and sky.

b. The naming of the sky.

> Again, ancient pagans worshiped the sun, the moon, the stars, and the sky—especially storms. Here, we learn that God created all these, and so reigns over them.[2]

Day 3 (vs. 9-13)

a. The gathering of the waters, revealing land.[3]

b. The naming of the waters and the land.

c. The land ordered to sprout vegetation and seed bearing plants, including trees.

> The land appears out of the waters, so there may have been a flood. The land sprouts plants, including

---

[2] Payne observes, "In pre-Christian Egypt confusion was introduced into biblical cosmology when the LXX [*Septuagint*, or Greek translation of the Hebrew Old Testament], perhaps under the influence of Alexandrian theories of a "stone vault" of heaven, rendered *rāqîa* by *stereōma* [steadfastness], suggesting some firm, solid structure. This Greek concept was then reflected by the Latin *firmamentum*, hence KJV "firmament." To this day non-believing critics wrongly claim the Hebrews thought the sky was solid, and supporting 'waters' above it." J. Barton Payne, "*raquia*, firmament" in Robert Laird Harris, *Theological Wordbook of the Old Testament*, 862.

[3] Many are unaware that all land used to be under water, according to geologists. Here, the text says God had to make the land appear. "The physical evidence geologists have gathered tells us that over a period of 4.56 billion years, Earth's landmass grew from 0 percent to 29 percent of the planetary surface." Hugh Ross, *Navigating Genesis: A Scientist's Journey through Genesis* (Covina CA: RTB Press, 2015) 54.

seed-bearing plants and trees—something that did not happen on the early earth, especially before marine life. We will discuss this discrepancy below.

After the creation of each class of living creature, Moses adds that they reproduce "after their kind." This suggests a limit to the amount of variation possible. But the word, "kind" is not defined.

Day 4 (vs. 14-19)

a. The creation (or appearance?) of the lights in the sky.

b. The naming of the lights.

As we will later see, most interpreters suggest that the sun and moon were already in existence, but are brought forward here for their naming. Hugh Ross observes, "Verse 16 tends to cause confusion for readers who fail to recognize it as a parenthetical note, or a brief review: God made two great lights—the greater light to govern the day and the lesser light to govern the night. He also made the stars."[4]

Some think the Sun and moon only became fully visible from earth at this time. But that explanation only works with certain readings, as we will see below.

The lights are literally "for signs and for seasons." This probably refers to the Hebrew festival calendar, not to the Zodiac or astrological calendar.[5]

Day 5 (vs. 20-23)

a. Creation of marine life of every kind and birds.

b. The blessing of the sea creatures and the birds.

---

[4] Ross, Hugh. *Navigating Genesis*, 62. He points out that in v. 18 the sun and moon are connected to the purpose echoing vs. 3 and 4, "to separate light from darkness." That strengthens the impression that 16 is parenthetical.

[5] Bruce Waltke, *Genesis*, 62.

Each time God blesses creatures, he gives them a commission to expand and prevail. It's similar to naming, and makes clear that animals got their powers from God.

Day 6 (vs. 24-31)

a. Calling the earth bring forth living creatures—animals.

b. Creation of humans.

c. The blessing and commissioning of humans.

> We examine this day in a subsequent chapter. The fact that the earth brings forth animals rather than God bringing them forth may be significant.

Day 7 (2:1-3)

a. Thus the heavens and the earth were completed, and all their hosts.

b. God completed His work... and He rested (2:2).

> Hebrews 4:3-5 makes clear that the reason God rested was not because he was tired, but because his work was finished, as you can also see from this verse. Artists usually stand back to admire and enjoy their work, just like this.

Interpretative approaches

Modern readers are quickly aware that the plain sense reading doesn't fit well with what we know about natural history. For instance, green, seed-bearing plants appear before marine life. That's way wrong. So is the creation of the Sun and moon on day 4 (vs. 16; 19). Science has the sun forming before the earth.

Bible-believing readers have developed several interpretations that attempt to reconcile all we know of natural history and the claims in Genesis.

Before wading into the interpretive question, we need to think about our method. How should we approach this question as Bible-believing followers of Jesus who are also educated in the findings of modern science?

The wrong way is to look at the possibilities, pick the one you think is right, and go out looking for evidence to back up that view. That's called "data mining," and it's a discredited approach.

When you already know your conclusion before you study the data, extreme bias will be the result. Inevitably, people using this method will end up minimizing or excluding data that doesn't fit their theory, while over-emphasizing points that are minor, but are suitable to their reading.

Too many Christians have adopted this approach.

Instead, we should come to this text admitting an important and undeniable point—we weren't there, and we don't know exactly what happened. What we have is a text that we believe is inspired and inerrant. But even inerrant texts have to be interpreted. And we have valid, credible findings from scientific research in natural history that must be addressed.

So the correct approach is to first find out what interpretations are possible—possible in that they don't violate the language or context. Other interpretations that violate biblical inerrancy should be discarded. That's because God *was* there. If this is his word, we can rely on it to be truthful.

We should rule out imposing genres, or modes of writing on the text that are non-historical when the text presents itself as historical.[6]

---

[6] I agree with "The Chicago Statement on Biblical Inerrancy," a document developed in 1978 and endorsed by virtually every conservative biblical scholar in America. In it, Article 18 says, "We affirm that the text of Scripture is to be interpreted by grammatico-historical exegesis, taking account of its literary forms and devices, and that Scripture is to interpret Scripture. We deny the legitimacy of

This will eliminate a number of proposed interpretations, but will not necessarily leave only one valid interpretation. Rather, we will end up with several interpretations that are permissible in that they fit within the text's range of meaning.

Here is where science comes in. If we have six views, and two of them contradict everything we know from science, we should discount those two views. We have no more reason to think God would mislead or deceive in his creative work than he would in inspiring scripture.

The big picture

By following this approach, we will be left with several views that don't necessarily contradict either science or scripture.

And then?

That's it. We're done. We don't need to determine which view is right, because that isn't possible. Neither is it necessary. It's enough to know what the basic message of the text is, and that it doesn't contradict known facts from science.

With this method in mind, let's consider several views.

---

any treatment of the text or quest for sources lying behind it that leads to relativizing, dehistoricizing, or discounting its teaching, or rejecting its claims of authorship." And, "We affirm that Genesis 1-11 is factual, as is the rest of the book. We deny that the teachings of Genesis 1-11 are mythical" (Article 22). Later came the "Chicago Statement on Biblical Hermeneutics," an equally important statement on interpretation. Article 13, states in part, "We deny that generic categories which negate historicity may rightly be imposed on biblical narratives which present themselves as factual." In other words, just because a telling of history employs poetic writing or refrains, doesn't mean we can discount the history being told. This position is based directly on the teaching of Jesus himself, who took these passages as historical and factual. In our church, we don't allow anyone to teach who doesn't agree with both of these statements in full.

6 Different Views of the Days

Genesis 1:2-31

Students of Genesis have arrived at several plausible explanations for the six days of creation. Here we look at some of the main views.

Gap Creation

> In the beginning God created the heavens and the earth. The earth was formless and void, and darkness was over the surface of the deep....
> (Genesis 1:1-2)

The *New International Version* (NIV) used to have a marginal note on the word "was" in the middle line. The alternative translation was "became." "The earth *became* formless and void." That translation suggests a gap of time between God's original creation and the six days in the rest of the chapter.

That could be the key to seeing how this passage fits into natural history. Perhaps God created the universe and later the earth, and then allowed the earth to age and develop over 4.5 billion years. He could have introduced multiple new life forms and let them evolve. The history of life would nearly all fit within this period.

Then, perhaps recently (4000 to 10,000 BC?), something bad happened. The earth became formless and void. If so, the six days of creation we read about in Genesis 1 might not be the original creation, but a recreation or renewal of what was here before.

This is the "gap theory" of creation. It used to be widely held among conservative scholars; according to evangelical theologian, Bernard Ramm,

> The gap theory has become the standard
> interpretation throughout hyper-orthodoxy,
> appearing in an endless stream of books, booklets,
> Bible studies, and periodical articles.[1]

Today, all that has changed. Gap creation is now a small, minority view. One reason is that crackpot supporters including cults like The Jehovah's Witnesses have discredited the view. Also, embellished versions of the gap theory, adding all kinds of strange, extra-biblical details, have caused confusion.[2]

The view lost some credibility when Early Gap Theorists mistakenly included Jer. 4:23-26 as describing the pre-Adamite world, when it clearly does not. The key section reads, "I looked at the earth, and it was empty (*bohu*) and formless (*tohu*)" (v. 23). But although it uses the *tohu bohu* vocabulary, the context involves the future Babylonian invasion of Israel, not creation. It was a classic case of word-association interpretation instead of contextual interpretation.[3]

The biggest reason for the decline of the Gap Theory is the upsurge of young earth creationism (discussed later). Their critiques are not convincing, especially when considering their alternative.

---

[1] Bernard Ramm, *The Christian View of Science and Scripture*, (Grand Rapids: Wm. B. Eerdmans Publishing Co. 1954) 135. Nicholas Matzke agrees, "Creationism that specifically argued, for a young Earth was relatively rare until the 1960s.... Most [Christian] leaders accepted some theory of Bible interpretation that allowed an old Earth, such as "Gap Theory." Nicholas J. Matzke, "The Evolution of Creationist Movements," *Evolution Education Outreach*, (2010) 3:145–162, 152.

[2] For instance A. J. Ferris's *The Conflict of Science and Religion*, (Vancouver: Association of the Covenant People, 1969) argued that some pre Adamic people survived and bred with Cain and later Ham to produce mongrel (colored) races. Others have argued that the pre-Adam race became angels. Isabella Duncan, *Pre-Adamite Man*, 1860.

[3] Early advocates also hung way too much weight on translating the first word in Genesis 1:2. They held that the "and" in the line, "and the world became formless and void," should read "but." That view is based on the Septuagint (Greek translation) and Latin versions which carry little weight. The point is that it doesn't matter and should not be part of the argument. The Gap Theory doesn't hang on that word.

But it's not up to a vote. The important question is whether the text allows for this reading, and it does.

God may have created original life, and for that matter, may have intervened at other points in natural history, all before the Gap event. Therefore, importantly, we can believe what we clearly see in the fossil record. So-called flood geology (see below) would not be the explanation for earth's geology and fossil record, under this view.

Humans?

Under the gap view it is possible that human-like creatures existed before the re-creation described in Genesis 1. Anthropological finds push the existence of homo sapiens back as far as 200,000 years. Related hominids date back to two million or more years. Under the gap reading, this could all be real, but all of it happened during a different, earlier period having nothing to do with our period. Whatever ended the previous created order is not revealed.

The gap view doesn't necessarily mean that everything on Earth died. Verses two and six make it sound like there was a flood; the land was under water. Some think this watery event might have corresponded to the end of the last ice age, about 10,000 years ago.

Others suggest a world flood that wiped out many, but not necessarily all, creatures; because such a complete elimination of all species has never happened as far as we can tell from the fossil record. A couple of worldwide extinction events have been very extensive, with over ninety percent of all live on land disappearing. But those were millions of years before humans existed.

Under this view, God's six creative days were probably replacing the lost species with the same or similar creatures, and repairing the ecosphere.

If there were human-like creatures before the gap, were they spiritual beings? We don't know. But they weren't humans, because 1 Corinthians 15:45 says Adam was the first man. They could have been similar to humans. Readers should be careful not to claim knowledge they don't have. It only says the earth became formless and void.

Could this event be related to the fall of Satan?

That's what many gap theorists believe, and it's possible. When Satan appears in Genesis 3 he's already fallen. Also, his fall as described in Ezekiel 28:11-19 includes the detail that he was "in Eden, the garden of God," *before* his fall (v. 13). So the anointed cherub, Satan, apparently had something to do with this planet, even before his fall from grace. Perhaps another Eden existed in the previous creation, and was also recreated here.

But a warning is in order: Gap Theorists have damaged this view by constructing and inserting elaborate scenarios about Satan, fallen angels, and pre-Adam people. Any correlation between Satan's fall and this passage is nothing more than a possibility. It's not important for judging the cogency of the view.

Problems with the gap theory

Some Hebrew students argue that translating Genesis 1:2 as "the earth *became* formless and void" violates usage of the Hebrew connecting word.[4] Other scholars disagree (compare with Genesis 19:26, where the same construction is properly translated this same way).

But the gap theory doesn't depend on the translation of this word. The fact that the earth was formless and void could, in itself, suggest that something went wrong. The world is a mess.

The main attack on the gap view of Genesis comes from young earth theologians (see below). They feel that allowing

---

[4] Most think the strongest critique of the Gap Theory comes from young earther, Weston W. Fields, *Unformed and Unfilled*, (Collinsville, IL: Burgener Enterprises 1976). I didn't find it persuasive and his alternative lacks credibility. It relies too heavily on the translation of v. 2 as mentioned above.

for billions of years under any scenario is compromising with the world and godless science.

This is a category mistake. Compromise applies to moral compromise with the world's values system, not with questions of truth. A proposition is either true or false, whether presented by a believer or a non-believer. You don't compromise with truth claims. You either agree with or deny the proposition.

If non-believing scientists demonstrate that the universe is billions of light-years in breadth, Christians have no reason to reject that, just because it came from a nonbeliever. Non-believing scientists can count, observe, compare, and analyze just like Christian scientists do. Of course they would have to show their evidence before we believe their findings. And we have to watch for bias.

The question before us is, which view best corresponds with the facts as we understand them so far? "The facts" here refer to the facts of scripture and the demonstrated facts of natural history.

The fact that the gap theory accords well with both natural history and with the text of Genesis is not compromise. Neither is it a discrediting factor. It's exactly what you would expect from a view that is true, and therefore it should be embraced as plausible.

Additional evidence

Besides the broad outline above, there are several other positives for this view.

- The gap theory accords well with the "evening and morning" language because the six days of creation may have been actual days. This is better than the questionable explanations in the day-age theory (see below).

- The word for "create" in verse 1 is *bara,* in the Qal form (in Hebrew, different forms often completely change the meaning). Harris et al. say of this, "The word is used in the Qal only of God's activity and is thus a purely theological term. This distinctive use of the word is especially appropriate to the concept of creation by divine fiat."[5] So, God wasn't working with existing material in the first line of verse 1. It must refer to the origin of the universe, and since it came from God, it must have been good. However, for the following days, he uses *hasha*, which means to fashion out of existing material.

- In the Old Testament, the words "formless and void" in verse 2 are associated with divine judgment. These are very negative words. *Tohu* means "laid waste" or "a wasteland" (Isaiah 24:10; 34:11; Jeremiah 4:23), or a place that has become desert (Deuteronomy 32:10). *Bohu* means a void, or emptiness (Jeremiah 4:23; Isaiah 34:11). These two verses and Genesis 1:2 are the only uses of *bohu* in the bible. Views that see nothing negative in this verse are ignoring the meaning of the words.[6]

- A major young earth argument against the Gap Theory is that the gap allows for death before the fall in Genesis 3. Most young earth theorists think physical death didn't exist before Genesis 3, even for animals. But the text doesn't make this claim. God's warning that death would ensue the day Adam ate of the forbidden fruit is predicting spiritual death for *humans*, not death for animals. He said "in the day that *you* eat of it, *you* will surely die." Young earthers claim that any death reflects sin and fallenness, but that doesn't accord with the fact that God is going to serve meat in heaven (e.g. Isaiah 25:6; 33:23).

---

[5] R. Laird Harris, Gleason Archer, and Bruce Waltke, *Theological Wordbook of the Old Testament,* [hereafter, TWOT] electronic ed., (Chicago: Moody Press, 1999) 127.

[6] Even Bruce Waltke, who is a framework theorist and rejects the gap theory, has a section on "The Negative State of Earth Before Creation." Bruce Waltke, *Genesis,* 59ff.

- If there is no gap after the first statement that God created the heavens and earth, it leaves a picture where God first created a negative mess and then sorted it out. Why would he do that? One possibility is that the mess is describing the primordial earth, still cooling, as the day-age theory argues. But it seems natural to see it as more negative than that.

- C. John Collins, an expert in Hebrew, points out that the verb, "created" in Genesis 1:1 is in the perfect tense, and the normal use of the perfect tense at the very beginning of a sequence is to denote an event that took place before the storyline gets underway.[7]

  John Lennox, commenting on this, argues that it shows that the question of the age of the earth (and of the universe) is a separate question from the interpretation of the days.[8]

- Isaiah 45:18 says,
  > For thus says the Lord, who created the heavens (He is the God who formed the earth and made it, He established it and did not create it a waste place [*tohu*], but formed it to be inhabited).

  As you can see, this verse declares that earth was not created formless. This again fits well the notion that it *became* formless sometime after original creation.

- 2 Peter 3:5 says,
  > ...God made the heavens by the word of his command, and he brought the earth out from the water and surrounded it with water. Then he used the water to destroy the ancient world with a mighty flood (NLT).

  But the last sentence is wrong in this translation. The correct reading is like the NIV and NASB:

---

[7] C. John Collins, *Genesis 1-4: A Linguistic, Literary, and Theological Commentary,* (Kindle Edition, 2011) Locations 582-584.

[8] John Lennox, *Seven Days That Divide the World: The Beginning According to Genesis and Science,* (Grand Rapids: Zondervan, 2011) 53.

> "Through which the world at that time was destroyed, being flooded with water."
>
> The phrase "at that time" is important—in context it refers to the time of creation. Most interpreters take this flood to refer to Noah's flood, but that would have been tens of thousands of years later. Even the young earth view has it thousands of years later. A destruction by water "at that time" could have been the catastrophe pictured in the gap view. Notice the language about God "brought the earth out from the water." That perfectly fits Genesis 1:6, which describes the land pushing up dividing the water.

The gap view of creation fits the facts of scripture and natural history. It sees the days of creation as literal days, which is preferable. This view could also be combined with the next view—the "days literal, but not sequential."

One of the main arguments against the Gap Theory is that it's too convenient. In other words, that it works out too well, suggesting it was made up. That's an invalid argument that should carry no weight. Fitting the data doesn't falsify a view. If the view fits the data, that suggests it could be true.

Days literal but not sequential theory

In this view, the days of creation describe several interventions by God with long gaps of time between the days. This periodic intervention by God is called "progressive creation." Progressive creation suggests that natural history is the result of a combination of creation and evolution. We will examine this in more detail below.

By accepting literal days, this view fits the "evening and morning" language better than views that see the days as long ages.

People holding this view typically don't see any gap between verse one and two, like those holding to the Gap Theory, although there's no reason they couldn't hold both views, perhaps resulting in the gap being further in the past.

The weakness of this view is that the order of the days doesn't match the progress of natural history. It has the earth created before the Sun, terrestrial plants before marine life, etc. Having millions of years between the days doesn't really help with this problem, but it does help with the "morning evening" language, because the days are literal.

Days representative

Some reply to this problem with the idea that the days are neither sequential nor chronological. They are merely representative days. That is, they are days given in an order different than what originally occurred—perhaps arranged thematically. This view is possible, though it seems like a stretch, and doesn't easily explain why the days are numbered.

Most progressive creation thinkers don't try to stipulate when or how many times God may have intervened. He may have intervened only a few times, or thousands of times. We simply don't know. The days given in Genesis 1 could be typical days, but there were other days as well. We know biblical authors are often selective in what they include, like all writers of history.

Critics complain that Exodus 20:11 rules out this view (and several others) by saying that the six days encompass the whole of creation,

> For in six days the Lord made the heavens and the earth, the sea and all that is in them, and rested on the seventh day; therefore the Lord blessed the Sabbath day and made it holy.

Those arguing for more than six days point out that Moses is just repeating the Genesis account here, and the issue of interpretation of the days is unaffected. What were the days? When did they occur? This passage doesn't say.

Some also note that the word for "made" here in Exodus is not *bara* like in Genesis 1:1, which means to create out of nothing. This word is *asah*, which means to fashion out of existing matter. So, they argue, this passage only describes the final result, not the whole process. Notice that the gap theory has no problem with this verse, because the long passage of time happened before the six days.

Progressive creation

Progressive creation is a view that can be joined to other views as a way to explain the fossil record in light of Genesis. It sees God's creative interventions spread out through natural history. This view accepts the data of geology and paleontology [the study of fossils] as real and the earth as billions of years old. But, while they believe evolution is real and explains much, more is needed. They believe that in addition to evolution, God intervened at multiple points to introduce new life forms, or even whole new levels of life complexity. Then, another period of evolution would result in further diversity.

Likely points for divine intervention include the original formation of life, the Cambrian explosion, and several other "explosions" of new life. An incredible leap forward in the complexity of life could signal God's intervention, and then variation and speciation between these events is the result of evolution.[9]

In this sense, progressive creation fits the fossil record better than naturalism or other views, because the fossil record does manifest surprisingly sudden appearances of new species and even families and phyla.[10]

---

[9] Günter Bechly et al. "The Fossil Record and Universal Common Ancestry" in J. P. Moreland, *Theistic Evolution*. They identify fifteen "explosions" or "radiations" in the fossil record where sudden leaps forward occurred. Each of these are big problems for Darwinian gradualism. They might signal intervention from God.

[10] John Lennox quotes David Raup of the Field Museum of Natural History, which houses one of the largest fossil collections in the world. "We are now about 120 years after Darwin and the knowledge of the fossil record has been greatly expanded. We now have a quarter of a million fossil species, but the situation hasn't changed much. The record of evolution is still surprisingly jerky and, ironically, we have even fewer examples of evolutionary transition than we had in Darwin's time.' Lennox, John *God's Undertaker* (p. 113). Staunch Darwin defender, Stephen Jay Gould, admits: "The absence of fossil evidence for

Atheist biologist, Richard Dawkins, discussing this problem admits,

> For example the Cambrian strata of rocks... are the oldest ones in which we find most of the major invertebrate groups. And we find many of them already in an advanced state of evolution, the very first time they appear. It is as though they were just planted there, without any evolutionary history.[11]

Progressive creation is compatible with other theories, including the day-age theory, the "days literal but not sequential" theory, and the "Gap Theory." As mentioned earlier, nothing in the text of Genesis requires that the days of creation be one immediately after the other, although that is the plain sense reading. Progressive creation is a superior view because it allows for earth's great age, clearly evident in the fossil record, astronomy, and geology (see below).

It makes sense that if God intervened into natural history to add additional creatures, he could also do that in a single day. He wouldn't need a long time to create by command. At the same time, there are good reasons why he would wait lengthy periods of time between creative acts, for instance, to allow time for the earth to become ready for the next step as we saw in the chapter on our planet.

Progressive creation is incompatible with theistic evolution, as we will see.

Day-age theory

We've already mentioned the day-age theory several times. Under this reading, each day is really a geological or cosmological age millions or even billions of years long. The

---

intermediary stages between major transitions in organic design... has been a persistent and nagging problem for gradualistic accounts of evolution." Stephen Jay Gould, "Is a New and General Theory of Evolution Emerging?" *Paleobiology* 6, No. 1 1980: 127.

[11] Richard Dawkins, *The Blind Watchmaker: Why the Evidence of Evolution Reveals a Universe without Design*, (New York: W. W. Norton, 1987), 229.

Hebrew word for "day" (*yom*) often refers to longer periods of time.

For example, Genesis 2:4 says, "This is the account of the heavens and the earth when they were created, in the day (*yom*) that the Lord God made earth and heaven." Here, the word day, in the singular, refers to the whole of chapter one.

Proponents of Day-Age sometimes hold to progressive creation as seen above. Others hold to theistic evolution, which we will examine below.

How do day-age proponents explain the "evening and morning" language? Leading author on the subject, Hugh Ross explains:

> Ancient Hebrew most often marked 24-hour days with 'evening to evening' and occasionally with 'morning to morning'." The "*… and was evening, and was morning*" phrase in Genesis 1 is unique thereby alerting "the reader that these days may have been periods other than 24-hour days.[12]

It's not very persuasive. The language remains a problem for this view. So do passages like Psalm 33:8–9: "Let all the earth fear the Lord; Let all the inhabitants of the world stand in awe of Him. For He spoke, and it was done; He commanded, and it stood fast." Doesn't this language make it sound like God was creating by fiat (decree), rather than by a gradual process?

A larger problem is that the days don't follow what we know about natural history. The problems are significant:

- The sun and moon aren't created until the fourth day. To this they answer, as some other views do, that the sun and moon already existed, but this is "perspectival language," or language from the view of someone on the surface of the earth. Before this, you couldn't see the sun or moon, because of the

---

[12] Hugh Ross, *A Matter of Days*, (Covina, CA: RTB Press 2nd ed.2004), 76.

primordial cloud layer covering the earth.

This response is very problematic, because the cloudy mantle around the earth ended long before vegetation appeared on land. This mantle was the result of the earth being so hot that all liquid water was evaporated.[13]

- Day three saw the creation of land plants, including seed-bearing plants. But according to the fossil record, seed bearing plants have only been with us for around 370 million years. At the same time, marine life doesn't come until day five. But the fossil record has marine life dating all the way back to 3.8 billion years. In reply, day-age theorists argue that the Hebrew has been mistranslated in verse 12. They claim it shouldn't read seed-bearing plants, and could actually refer to microscopic life.[14]

We conclude that the day-age view has significant problems in aligning the days with eras in natural history.

Days of revelation

According to this theory, the days are not days of creation, but days of revelation.[15] Proponents of this view argue that while Moses was with God on the mountain, or some other time, he was shown a series of seven visions, one each day. He then recorded a synopsis of what he saw day by day in Genesis.

---

[13] Notice that the gap theory doesn't have this problem. In the gap view, the sun and moon would have been obscured probably only for a matter of days. Instead of the mantle caused by the molten surface of early earth, the sky would have merely been cloudy from the destructive flood that destroyed the world.

[14] Ross says, "A team of paleontologists uncovered extensive fossil evidence for nonmarine (i.e., non-ocean-dwelling) eukaryotic life-forms (i.e. having cell nuclei) that date back as early as 1.2 billion years ago. That would be far earlier than scientists thought land-based organisms arose. But still not far back enough to match the appearance of the Sun and moon. Hugh Ross, *Navigating Genesis*, 58.

[15] First articulated by P. J. Wiseman, *Creation Revealed in Six Days*, (London: Marshall, Morgan & Scott, 1948) 144.

The problem with this view is that nothing in the text signals that these are visions. Normally prophets say, "I saw the Lord sitting on a throne..." (Isaiah 6:1), or "In the first year of Belshazzar king of Babylon Daniel saw a dream..." (Daniel 7:1), or something similar. In other words, the writer announces or gives a cue that this part is a vision. In Genesis 1 we have no such cue. So, while this "days of revelation" could have happened, we have no reason in the text to think it did.

For that reason, the view ends up assigning a non-historical genre (visions) for what presents itself as historical (see below on inerrancy). Of course, God no doubt did reveal these days to Moses, as he did the following chapters. But it seems a stretch to assign the numbering of the days to refer to the numbering of his visions.

Followers of this view have declined into a small minority in our day.

The big picture

One important point for walking believers is that we have several possible ways to account for the harmony of the text of Genesis 1 and natural history. As we argued at the beginning of the chapter, we don't need to determine which one is right, and indeed, we cannot. But fact that there is no necessary contradiction between proven secular findings and biblical teaching is important to scientifically trained readers.

Bernard Ramm was right when he observed of Genesis 1, "The time element and the causal element are so completely the tool and instrument of the Divine Will that they are ignored in the *theological expressions* of creation."[16] This text is primarily teaching on the power and transcendence of God. It shows that the creation is unworthy of worship (which was the norm in ancient times) because God is the origin of all.

---

[16] Bernard Ramm, *The Christian View of Science and Scripture,*" 150.

But, it also uses language that is sequential and refers to days, mornings, and evenings. And any valid view has to give some account for those terms.

We also have scientific findings that are beyond question, dwell.

7 Unacceptable Theories

Some interpretations of the six days, including Bible-believing views, are unacceptable. These views either violate the inspiration of the text, use an approach other than the grammatical-historical method, or contradict well-established scientific facts. Although these are not the only examples, we will cover the three most popular views that exemplify the problem.

Young earth creation

Proponents of the young earth theory of creation believe the text of Genesis 1 allows for nothing but six literal days, each following immediately after the other, and that the whole episode happened not long ago—perhaps six to ten thousand years ago. The date is based on the generations in Genesis. According to this view, not only the earth, but the universe itself is only a few thousand years old. They deny the big bang and all the evidence behind it.

When critics confront young earth theorists with the fossil record or geological signs of great age for the earth, young earth theorists claim that most of these are the result of the world flood in Genesis 6-8.

This so-called "flood geology" argues that the flood destroyed most life on earth, and stirred up soil and other debris because of rushing water. Then, as the waters subsided, these bones, shells, and debris settled into today's fossil record. Young earth readers have a scenario that they feel explains why fossils are sorted out they way they are based on density and size.

In some cases, young earthers resort to an "apparent age" argument. According to this argument, when, for instance, God created Adam he was an adult, even when he was only one minute old. Similarly, when creating a planet or a universe, they would look old even the first day they existed, but it's only apparent age.

Unfortunately, the young earth view of creation is entirely discredited and should be dismissed by thoughtful Christians.

Key weaknesses:

1. Young earth interpreters are mistaken when they insist Genesis can only be understood as spanning a few thousand years. We have already seen several readings that honor the text and allow for great age.

2. Their methodology is wrong. Instead of studying the text to determine the outer limits of fair interpretation, young earthers engage in data mining. They start with their conclusion and then dip into scientific findings only far enough to find confirming evidence.

3. No good explanation has been given for the fossil record. Flood geology suggests that heavy organisms, like shellfish, would sink to the bottom first. Mammals would float for a time and then sink, ending up near the top of the sediment stack.

   This is a completely inadequate explanation for what we seen in the fossil record. Fossils reveal that billions of years passed with only single cell organisms. Then, as larger organism begin appearing half a billion years ago, the fossils at the bottom contain only archaic long-gone species, slowly progressing to more recent species and finally modern animals like those we see today.

   In other words, it is their species that determines where fossils form, not their size or density. There is no reason why a flood of rushing water would result in this kind of sorting out.

4. Sediments formed in moving water, like those from flooding or alluvial fans (formed when rivers reach a plane at the base of a mountain range, or when rivers reach the ocean), are completely different from slowly deposited sediments produced in still water like lakes and oceans. It's easy to recognize sediments deposited rapidly by moving water. Many types of sediment, like gypsum or limestone, only form very slowly, never in a matter of months or a year.

5. The "apparent age" argument could have application for the few years of apparent age with Adam. But when young earthers apply it to the vast age of earth and the universe, this argument ends up implying that God is a deceiver.

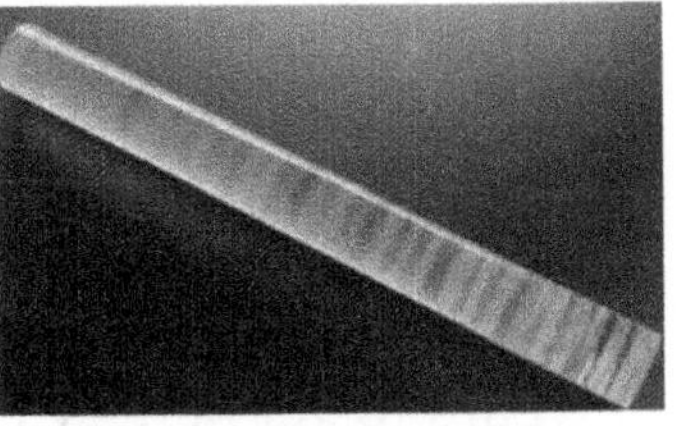

Take, for example, polar ice cores. Scientists have been drilling and studying ice cores from Greenland and other polar regions for decades.

When you look at one of the cores, you see it is striped. That's because summer and winter produce different amounts of ice and some melting. Here's the point: these ice cores extend thousands of feet, with over six hundred thousand annual cycles recorded.

A young earth theorist might argue that God wanted to create the earth with polar ice caps already in place, and that's possible. But why would he have them striped, six hundred thousand layers deep? It serves no functional purpose.

To claim that God made the ice caps this way implies that God is deceptive. What other reason would there be for God to recently create ice caps that look far older? This position is theologically and scientifically untenable. God is no more deceiving in his works than in his words.

Another example involves coral atolls. Corals are living organisms that secrete calcium-based scaffolding where the organisms can live protected from predators.

Coral reefs add less than an inch a year. But we have coral atolls that extend thousands of feet down from the ocean surface. In other words, these atolls are hundreds of thousands to millions of years old.

No one can claim corals used to grow at a different rate, because these are living organisms with fixed abilities. Their annual markings show how long they have lived. Neither could these atolls be created by flood geology. Any objective observer must conclude that the earth is far older than young earthers say.

Some stars are a billion or more light years away from earth. But we see their light that took a billion years to get here. Young earth apparent age apologists claim that God created the stars with their light already on its way to earth. This again suggests that God is a deceiver.[1]

I think young earth creationism has been an absolute disaster for the cause of Christ in our times. Christians holding this view are often persuaded by their leaders that it's the only view that's faithful to scripture. But it really announces to the world that to be a Christian you have to avert your eyes from valid science, and that God might be a trickster creating things that look different than they really are.

---

[1] Some earlier young earthers even suggested that the speed of light might have been faster earlier! But even if light traveled, for some unknown reason, at twice the speed it does today, these stars would still be billions of years old. This approach has largely been abandoned. Gerald Aardsma, Institute for Creation Research "Has the Speed of Light Decayed?," *Impact* May 1988.

Proponents of the framework hypothesis argue that the days in Genesis 1 are not historical, but conceptual—that each day makes up part of the literary frame around the main subject.

These theorists compare verses 1-3 to 4-6, as seen to the right. They argue that each kingdom on the left was subsequently populated with a matching "creature kind" (even though the sun and moon are not creatures).

Creation Kingdoms	Creature Kinds
Day 1: Light	Day 4: Luminaries
Day 2: Sky/Water	Day 5: Birds/Fish
Day 3: Land/Vegetation	Day 6: Land animals/Man
The Creator King	
Day 7: Sabbath	

The seventh day is lacking the morning and evening language, so it's in a different category.

The problem with this theory is that it doesn't treat Genesis 1 as normal history. Instead, it's a fairly vague affirmation that God was behind it all. Since it makes no specific claims about days or when different things were created, this view is fully compatible with theistic evolution.

The idea that the days in Genesis could be arranged topically instead of chronologically is less objectionable in itself. Ancient writers didn't share the modern insistence on sequence and chronological precision. Students of the Gospels find that some gospel writers gather Jesus' words or deeds into a thematic arrangement. But here the days are numbered, and that's a problem for this view. So is the "morning and evening" language.

The framework approach is arguably not grammatical historical interpretation. It relies on literary analysis that is quite subjective. The categories don't line up that well. Notice that water is not created on the second day, but is already there on the first, "The Spirit of God was hovering over the face of the waters" (v. 1:2). Also, the plants are created on day 3, but they should be "filling" the land, and so would be on day 6 according to this scenario.

It's hard to believe that this is actually what the author had in mind or what ancient readers would have seen.[2] In fact, it's a recent theory, unknown in theology before a Dutch theologian propounded it in 1927.[3]

Notwithstanding the fact that a number of prominent Bible-believing scholars hold to this view (e.g., Kent Hughes, Tim Keller, Bruce Waltke, Meredith Kline, Gordon Wenham, and many others),[4] I think it runs afoul of the earlier comments about the definition of inerrancy by assigning a non-historical genre to historical narrative.

True literary structure

A more plausible analysis of the literary pattern is this—throughout Genesis, the text covers the flow of history over a period like here with the six days. In later chapters it's the generations, or genealogies.

Then, at multiple points, the text stops to examine in detail the last part of the sequence—in this case, day 6 and the creation of humans covered in Chapter 2. At each stopping point, Moses says, "this is the account" or similar. The word for "account" in Hebrew is "*toledot.*"

Toledot can be translated "generations," but it's really the family story for the person in question. Moses divides the book of Genesis by *toledot* formula as follows:

---

[2] Hughes, himself a framework reader, admits, "It [Genesis 1] is not poetry but narrative prose. The whole account is written in the normal Hebrew narrative tense. Hughes, R. Kent. Genesis: *Beginning and Blessing,* (Wheaton: Crossway), 25. Historical narratives in Hebrew are characterized by waw-consecutive verbs like here in Genesis 1. Compare the narrative telling in Genesis 1 with the poetic account of creation in Psalm 104 to see the difference.

[3] Dr. Arie Noordzij of the University of Utrecht's paper, *God's Word en der Eeuwen Getuigenis,* was the first proponent of the Framework Hypothesis in 1924.

[4] Probably the first and most important paper on framework is Meredith G. Kline, "Space and Time in the Genesis Cosmogony," *Perspectives on Science and Christian Faith* 48 (March 1996). Opponents of framework are also respected. They include Andrew Steinmann, Robert McCabe, Wayne Grudem, and Millard Erickson.

History of the heavens and the earth (2:4b-4:26)

History of Adam (5:1-6:8)

History of Noah (6:9-9:26)

History of the sons of Noah (10:1-11:9)

History of Shem (11:10-26)

History of Terah (11:27-25:11)

History of Ishmael (25:12-18)

History of Isaac (25:19-35:29)

History of Esau (36:1-8 and 36:9-42)

History of Jacob (3 7:1-50:26)

For each one, the first verse contains the word, "*toledot.*"

This is the true literary pattern throughout Genesis, and it shows that chapter one and two have the same literary structure as the rest of Genesis, and therefore should be viewed as history, just like the rest of the book—not as a different conceptual "framework."[5]

Proponents of framework are well aware of the *toledot* structure of Genesis. Yet, they see the sequence in Chapter 1—with its evening-morning language and numbering of the days from one to seven—as different than later stories.

Theistic evolution

Proponents of this view accept the claims of naturalistic science completely or nearly so. The main problem with theistic evolution is trying to find the "*theo*" (God) in the view. It should more correctly be called *deistic* evolution. Under deism, God started the clock and walked away, never intervening again.

---

[5] Framework supporters dwell on the "evening and morning" formula as somehow signaling the shift to a poetic or otherwise non-sequential, non-historical narrative. But this formula doesn't really point to a framework. Arguably, it far more suggests a temporal sequence.

Some of them make general claims that God might have somehow "guided" evolution but never flesh those claims out. Instead, they attack any view that God periodically intervened to introduce new life forms. Most theistic evolutionists maintain that God only created the conditions that he knew would lead to evolution, thus justifying the claim that God created.

Some theistic evolutionists allow for one or two intrusions by God—usually, but not always, at the origin of life, and the modification of humans to include a non-material soul.

But leading thinkers in this school warn not to attribute things to God at all, because you might make a "Galileo mistake." This refers to times when the church denied valid scientific findings that later prove undeniable, thus heaping disgrace on the church. That is a valid worry, although theistic evolutionists go too far. Our guiding light should be what the text says, not avoiding a possible overstep.

They also argue that if people point to major change events like the Cambrian explosion and say God intervened there, it's a "God of the gaps" argument. In this kind of argument you attribute anything we don't understand yet to God. God becomes only the God of the gaps, a God whose domain is ever shrinking, as we learn more, while generating embarrassment for believers.

To this, we should point out that anyone who believes in answered prayer or any other divine intervention also believes in gaps that are the result of God's intervention. Just because some have wrongly attributed a natural event to God's intervention in the past, doesn't justify never again seeing God's hand in history.

Nearly all theistic evolutionists think the first chapters of Genesis are non-historical. The idea of God fashioning Adam personally has no place in this view, neither does his fashioning of Eve. Rather, Adam was part of a community of early humans, numbering at least in the thousands. Adam and Eve are just symbolic of humanity in general.

This is clearly wrong. Paul says everyone got their fallen nature from "one man" (Romans 5:12).[6]

Most theistic evolutionists think God selected an already existing creature, Homo Sapiens, and imbued him with a soul. That leads to dismissing the creation of Eve from Adam's side. Very few accept that account and hold that God also imbued her with a soul.

This scenario is theoretically possible, if they hold that all subsequent humans came from Adam and Eve, eventually outlasting any other Homo Sapiens. Again, Paul says, "through *one man* sin entered into the world, and death through sin..." (Romans 5:12). This plain statement rules out the idea that many humans did not descend from Adam.

I think it's extremely unlikely that any such co-opting of an existing human happened, for several reasons:

- Humans stand at an astonishing distance from any other animal in intellect and a number of other features. This gulf—detailed in a later chapter—is unlike anything found elsewhere in nature. There is no example of any creature exhibiting such a dramatic superiority to all other species in any capability. This weighs powerfully against gradual evolution as a sufficient explanation for humans.

- It's clear that God intervened by imbuing Adam with a soul, so this view fails to remove the need for divine intervention—one of its main reasons for existing.[7]

---

[6] There is an argument from Population Genetics that humans were never fewer ten thousand at the time they diverged from Chimpanzees. But the argument is flawed for several reasons. See Ann K. Gauger, Ola Hössjer, and Colin R. Reeves "Evidence for Human Uniqueness," in J. P. Moreland, et al. *Theistic Evolution: A Scientific, Philosophical, and Theological Critique*, (Wheaton: Crossway, 2017). This is an important book written by well qualified scholars. It thoroughly dismantles theistic evolution.

[7] This is Francis Collins' basis for advancing theistic evolution. He says, "Faith that places God in the gaps of current understanding about the natural world may be headed for crisis if advances in science subsequently fill those gaps." And one of the gaps he includes is the origin and spirituality of humans. Francis S. Collins, *The Language of God*, 93.

- The plain reading of Genesis 1 and 2 indicates Adam and Eve were alone and no other humans were around. The view that there were thousands of other humans comes from secular science, not from the text of Genesis. The burden of proof lies with anyone who thinks the plain reading is wrong.

- Genesis 2 has God directly creating Eve, thus again robbing theistic evolution of its reason for existence—that is, creating a scenario without any need for direct intervention by God. Most theistic evolutionists simply discount the story as metaphor. Obviously, if there were thousands of women already in existence, there would be no need to create another.

The big picture

We have well-fitting options on how to read Genesis 1 that do no violence to scripture or to natural history. Therefore, we have no reason to turn aside to these unacceptable theories.

8 Evolution and Genesis

Extreme positions

The traditional debate over evolution is that either creation or evolution accounts for all of Earth's natural history. It's either all evolution or no evolution. In large measure, that still tends to be the choice given readers.

At one extreme is secular science with their insistence on universal common descent. With the same or similar view we have biologos.com, a Christian group of thinkers committed to theistic evolution. They see no problem with any part of the secular scenario, and spend most of their time attacking Christian conservatives rather than attacking atheistic evolution.

At the other extreme is creation research, advancing young earth creationism and categorically rejecting evolution except at the most microscopic level.

In my opinion, neither of these extremes are necessary. There is no reason why evolution and creation could not coexist.

A more moderate group at discovery.com focuses on intelligent design without committing to any particular interpretive approach. However, even some of them seem to have problems with the idea of evolution across the board. They have done good work showing how unlikely it is that Darwinian evolution can account for major new levels of information.

Evolution is an established process that accounts for much of life as we know it. And God's handiwork isn't diminished at all by the idea that he created a molecular system capable of adapting to new conditions with new versions of DNA coding. At the same time, evolution cannot, by itself, account for all we see in the history of life.

Clear backing for evolution

While origin of life is impossible without a creator, that doesn't lead to the conclusion adopted by many theists— that evolution is therefore a phony construct, and isn't real.

Evolution accounts well for certain types of adaptation and change especially at a given level of complexity. For instance, consider examples of evolution we have seen in our own lifetimes, such as DDT resistant insects or antibiotic resistant bacteria. Some of these are new species, while others are altered species who now pass their immunity to their offspring via altered DNA. That's evolution, happening right before our eyes.

So too, frequently cited examples like the evolution of the horse from earlier, smaller forms is quite plausible and relatively well documented.[1] These are examples of minor evolution rather than major evolution. The different iterations of the horse aren't radically different, but involve change in size and minor skeletal features, or, in the case of antibiotic resistance, changes in the organism's biochemistry.[2]

Life forms on isolated islands (like Australia) invariably differ greatly from life forms on connected continents, and evolution is the best explanation for those differences. Think here about kangaroos, wombats, or other marsupials unique to Australia, but also thousands of other examples on various islands. Any suggestion that God decided to create different species only on each isolated island again would imply that God is a deceiver.

Christians have no reason to deny evolution in these or many other cases.

---

[1] This is common knowledge.
https://en.wikipedia.org/wiki/Evolution_of_the_horse

[2] I think the term "micro evolution" should be discarded. "Micro" is a poor descriptor for the extent of evolution evident in the fossil record. It's much more than that. But universal common descent is not demonstrated in the fossil record either.

Consider the difference between the idea of "common descent" and the idea of "universal common descent." The first is describing two or more species that shared a common ancestor. The salt water and fresh water crocodile probably go back to a shared ancestor. How is that a threat to anything biblical?

The notion of *universal* common descent on the other hand, is an unproven faith claim: a dogma. How could anyone know that all species have descended from a single source? The fossil record doesn't demonstrate that. The only reason for adopting the universal descent dogma is a faith commitment to naturalism—the nonexistence of a creating God.

Naturalists claim that analysis of genetic codes point to universal common descent. But that conclusion is based on unproven assumptions. Is similarity in some segments of DNA the result of common descent? Or is it the result of a common creator?

First, it's very surprising that all life on earth now and throughout history is based on the same, single genetic code. While everything else is evolving wildly, this code basically doesn't change at all. This points to creation assumptions—that similarity of design points to the same creator—more than to atheistic assumptions—that similarity in design points to common ancestry. Undirected modification should have resulted in far more variation in how the code of life works.

Why would a master designer create vastly different DNA codes for similar features? For instance, DNA that codes for hair is going to look very similar, regardless of the species. We see this in software design. Programmers don't write every section of code from scratch. They write some new code, but also have libraries of routines that can be combined as needed in the creation of a new program.

This is a perfectly plausible explanation for the similarities we see over sections of code between mammals, reptiles, etc. It also could explain cases where identical strings of DNA code are found at different places in the genome for different species.

Junk DNA

"Junk DNA" is the term for lengthy stretches in our genome that don't code for proteins, and appeared to be nonsense when discovered. Atheistic and Theistic evolutionists were quick to declare that these meaningless sections were trash left over from failed mutations earlier in evolutionary history. Such junk is what one might expect from an unguided process of evolution.

That impression was strengthened when scientists discovered matching sections of junk DNA in, for instance, mice and humans. Since they don't code for anything, the only explanation must be that mice and humans have a shared ancestor. Theistic evolutionist Francis Collins argued in his book, *The Language of God*, that because of matching junk DNA, "the conclusion of a common ancestor for humans and mice is virtually inescapable."[3]

Later, this turned out to be an example of ideology choking out open-minded research. Today most "junk DNA" has proven to be far from junk. Every section of these long sequences are now known to carry out essential control operations, governing gene expression and a host of other operations in the cell.[4]

Limitations to evolution

In Genesis 1:12, 21, 24, 25 we read that each category of plants or animals reproduce, "after its own kind." This argues that universal common descent is unbiblical. There

---

[3] Francis Collins, *The Language of God*, 136– 137.

[4] For a short explanation see "'Junk' DNA Has Important Role, Researchers Find," ScienceDaily (May 21, 2009). Or for a complete technical explanation see Jonathan Wells, *The Myth of Junk DNA*, (Seattle: Discovery Institute Press, 2011).

must have been some limit to how much a given type of creature could differ from its original ancestor. However, the word 'kind' is not defined. It could mean species, genus, family, or even something larger, like orders or phyla. But the fact remains that "Reproducing after its own kind" has to mean *something*. Theistic evolution readers ignore this fact, and embrace universal common descent.

The fossil record

The fossil record reveals the likelihood of extensive evolution. However, it does not match well with the doctrine of universal, gradual, common descent. A huge problem remains: strata containing abundant fossil remains from entire new orders lie immediately adjacent to strata containing none of these organisms or anything similar. That suggests the sudden appearance of new categories of animals and plants—a scenario that fits progressive creation but not gradual modification through mutations.

To claim (as naturalistic and theistic evolutionists do) that every species on earth and throughout history has evolved from only one individual or group of original organisms is a very bold and broad claim. It's also very fragile. A single counter example would falsify this view. On its face, it is philosophical and faith-based. It assumes what has not been demonstrated.

When scientists proclaim universal common descent, they are not looking for truth. They are starting with a position that requires all data to be interpreted in one way. They are by definition, not open to any alternative. They are ironically much like young earthers in this respect. They are unscientific.

Again, we have no evidence from the fossil record to support the broad claim that all species descended from one ancestor. Our evidence for evolution is limited to much narrower examples of common ancestry. New species often spring into existence in the fossil record with no known intermediary or predecessor. Most persist with little change during their existence. Then, they disappear.[5]

The mechanism of neodarwinian evolution involves mutations at the molecular level in DNA. Only tiny changes have any chance of success. Larger mutations invariably result in handicapped specimens or death—and naturalistic scientists agree with this observation.

But the fossil record reflects many quite sudden, massive changes that don't fit this picture. Extraordinary leaps forward, like the Cambrian explosion, have been compressed by recent findings to a much shorter time than earlier thought. Yet the changes are massive, including the origin of most animal phyla still alive today. How this happened in such a short time remains one of the great mysteries in natural history. But naturalists still insist that only one solution is possible—blind chance.

Naturalists claim that the predecessors to these large, often bony creatures existed, but simply failed to leave fossils behind. Yet, delicate sponge embryos with soft bodies are preserved in the rock immediately below the Cambrian explosion.[6] To insist on the existence of invisible missing fossils reflects faith, not scientific objectivity.

The big picture

Christians shouldn't deny evolution. Neither should anyone deny creation. The evidence strongly suggests a combination of natural and supernatural events working together. God worked this all out, slowly readying the planet over four billion years.

---

[5] John Lennox, *Seven Days that Divide the World: The Beginning According to Genesis and Science*, (Grand Rapids: Zondervan, 2011), 113. This excellent book from a top flight scientist and mathematician is a great read for anyone struggling with this question.

[6] Jennifer Frazer "What the Heck Are These Fossils?" *Scientific American*, May 23, 2019.

None of this contradicts a fair reading of Genesis or anything actually demonstrated in the natural history of earth.

The Christian worldview, as articulated by Francis Schaeffer is "Uniformity of cause and effect in an open system." Yes, cause and effect are real, and natural processes function according to natural laws put in place by God. Therefore, we can explore the world discovering cause and effect relationships without doubting our findings.

Yet, the system is also open, which means God can intervene. Anyone who believes in prayer or in Jesus' incarnation agrees with that. But most of the time, God has constructed nature so that it functions without any need for constant intervention. At the same time, the forces in nature that make the universe work are all sustained by God. So in that sense, he is constantly upholding it.

Not spiritualism or animism

The idea that everything that happens in the world is directly caused by God is not the Christian view. That view is spiritualism or animism. Such a view renders science pointless, and is really antithetical to all scientific thinking. What's the point in studying natural systems when the real reason for everything is God?

God does rule over the world, but being sovereign doesn't mean he has to directly cause everything, even though he could if he wanted to. Instead, he set up a system, a universe with physical forces that work just so.

The Big Picture

For all these reasons and more besides, Christian thinkers should be perfectly comfortable seeing natural cause and effect sequences along with periodic divine intervention. Progressive creation is highly probable. Evolution and creation work together without any contradiction.

9 Humans Arrive

Genesis 1:26-2:

Humans are the punch line of the creation story. In Genesis 1 we read,

> Then God said, "Let us make man in our image, according to our likeness; and let them rule over the fish of the sea and over the birds of the sky and over the cattle and over all the earth, and over every creeping thing that creeps on the earth."
>
> God created man in his own image, in the image of God he created him; male and female He created them.
>
> God blessed them; and God said to them, "Be fruitful and multiply, and fill the earth, and subdue it; and rule over the fish of the sea and over the birds of the sky and over every living thing that moves on the earth." (vs. 26-28)

The triune God

When God says, "Let us make man in our image," why is he speaking in the plural? Some interpreters argue that he is talking to the angels, who were present at creation (Job 38:6-7). But scripture nowhere suggests that angels could create. They were bystanders.

Jewish interpreters argue that it's the royal "we" speaking for the commonwealth. But that doesn't fit this setting well, because he isn't addressing others, but himself.

God is triune, and he is here pictured speaking to "himselves." The word for God here (*elohim*) is also plural, and so throughout the Hebrew Bible.[1]

In God's image

To be created in the image of God—what does it mean? It's nothing to do with our appearance. The point is that humans were created at a very high order, similar in some ways to God. Humans are personal, spiritual beings. This separates them from every other life form on earth, as you can clearly see from this passage. It also flatly contradicts all naturalistic theories of human origin and nature, because no physical process like evolution could ever result in this non-material God-like image.

Creation in the image of God is one of the most important concepts in the Bible, and one of the deepest. It governs our understanding in many areas, from ethics, to the afterlife, to the nature of God and to our relationship with him.

God's nature

To understand what the image of God means, we can carefully read about humans before they fell from God's will. Since they were created in his image, studying humans should tell us some things about God.

Additional information surfaces during and after the fall, but everything is somewhat distorted after the fall. So the material from before the fall is most important.

---

[1]The Old Testament teaches the Trinity, just like the New. For instance, see Isaiah 61:1, "The Spirit of the Lord God (*Yahweh Elohim*) is upon me." Notice Jesus read this passage in Luke 4:18-21, concluding that, "Today this Scripture has been fulfilled in your hearing." In other words, he claimed to be the "me" in this passage—the Messiah. That makes sense, because the one speaking in this passage goes on to bring in happiness, rebuild Jerusalem, bring in world peace, and everlasting joy. But in the same context in Isaiah 61, he goes on to say, "For I, the Lord (*Yahweh*), love justice...etc." So the "me" in verse 1 is *Yahweh* in verse 8. It's the triune God—"The *Spirit* of the *Lord God* (*Yahweh Elohim*) is upon me (also *Yahweh*)." You can see the trinity again in Isaiah 48, where the same one who says in verse 12, "I am He, I am the first, I am also the last," goes on to say in verse 16, "The Lord God (*Yahweh Elohim*) has sent Me, and His Spirit."

Each feature we find in the original humans corresponds with something in God's nature. So as we study unfallen humans, we learn about God.

Ideals for today and later

These elements in human nature not only spell out what God wanted humans to be back then, they also point to what God still wants people to be today. His design for humanity was good, and he hasn't abandoned it. When Jesus returns and history as we know it comes to an end, humanity will return to what we were designed to be. That means we can study unfallen humanity to learn about what we will be like in heaven.

But not only will we reacquire these features in heaven, we can begin reacquiring them now. Under the life-changing power of the Holy Spirit, Christians can immediately begin moving back toward what we were designed to be.

The big picture

The features found in humans before the fall away from God are like a blueprint for fulfillment, purpose, and happiness. It's important to scrutinize each of these features carefully to understand more about God, more about ourselves as we should be, and more about awaits us in heaven.

So what were humans before the fall?

10 Humans Lead and Are Significant
Genesis 1:26

In Genesis 1:26 God created humans and stipulated that they have a key feature, "Let Us make man in Our image, according to Our likeness; *and let them rule...*" (emphasis added).

Humans were created to be active agents of change, protection, and provision for the world.

God is a leader

God is a kind, powerful, and loving leader. He created the world, and he owns it, and everything and everybody in it (Psalm 24:1). That's why he deserves to be followed—a trait called sovereignty.

God is sovereign by nature. He doesn't use his sovereignty in a way that contradicts his other attributes, like goodness and love. Rather, he leads his creation for its own good. Creatures who follow God's lead end up with better, healthier, and happier lives.

Those who deny and reject God's sovereignty destroy their own lives, and end up under his judgment. His judgment falls because he cannot ignore such a terrible and sinful act as the judge of the universe.

God is a giver. He knows his leadership is benevolent and through leading the universe he can supply what they need. He always acts and leads for the benefit of his creatures.

People as significant leaders

God did not create humans to be passive observers of their world, or to drift with the current. He made us to be powerful, creative agents of change, protection, and care. Whenever we read about godly leadership in the Bible, we see leadership that is not for self-advantage, but to benefit those being led.

Jesus decried what he considered the spirit of the Gentiles:

> You know that those who are recognized as rulers of the Gentiles lord it over them; and their great men exercise authority over them. But it is not this way among you, but whoever wishes to become great among you shall be your servant; and whoever wishes to be first among you shall be slave of all. For even the Son of Man did not come to be served, but to serve, and to give His life a ransom for many. (Mark 10:42-45)

This critical distinction is at the center of what God had in mind for humans. Not that we exploit the world for selfish advantage, but that we serve the world and other people in it, and try to make it better, that we take care of the world as stewards.

Unlike with God, leading doesn't come to us by virtue of our creating the world. Rather, our leadership was delegated to us by God in the verse in question—"let them rule."

He repeated his intent after creating Adam,

> God blessed them; and God said to them, "Be fruitful and multiply, and fill the earth, and subdue it; and rule over the fish of the sea and over the birds of the sky and over every living thing that moves on the earth. (Genesis 1:28)

Again, the word here translated "rule" is simply the governmental word used in that day for a king's or queen's leadership of his or her country. It doesn't imply domination or tyranny. God himself is a great king, and he's not a tyrant (Malachi 1:14).

Postmodern critics and others claim that this passage pits humans against nature, and advances a vision where humans can destroy entire ecosystems at will. But that was never God's intent.

Under the biblical view of delegated leadership, under-leaders are always responsible to do what is best for their following, and to carry out their overlord's will. They are also fully accountable to God, their superior. This is true of Old Testament and the New Testament according to Jesus (Matthew 24:45-51).

Reclaiming significance

We will examine later how this feature of humans was distorted after their fall from God's will.

The good news is that we can substantially reclaim our place as significant leaders under God. Besides caring for their own families and the earth, humans are in a position to powerfully advance God's agenda for this world. And when doing so, we gain a gratifying sense of significance and purpose that has a wholesome, uplifting effect on our souls. Those who lead for self-gratification also receive a lift when they lead, but it's not healthy or nurturing, and that's why they constantly feel the need for more.

Advancing God's agenda begins with following his will for one's self, and moves to teaching his will to each person's family. From there, we can reach further out to the people of God, building up our Christian community. Then, we can reach further still to reach people who don't know God with the gospel. And we can reach out to heal, and to care for the poor and needy.

Working together with the people of God, humans feel gratified and happy as they advance God's purposes and his word in the power of the Holy Spirit. This is what we were created for.

In heaven

Heaven is not a place of passive existence with no purpose. Such a place would be closer to hell for creatures like us with architectures that insist on accomplishing important goals.

Instead, we read that our future with God includes cities, a society, and the never-ending quest to understand and know God more deeply. Jesus said that when the king passes judgment, he tells those who are good stewards, "I will put you in charge of many things" (Matthew 25:21 see also 24:47). He promises his disciples that they will "sit upon twelve thrones, judging the twelve tribes of Israel" (Matthew 19:28).

In the parable of the minas, Jesus has the nobleman tell the faithful servants, "You have been faithful in a very little thing, you are to be in authority over ten cities" (Luke 19:17).

We know that we will never cease breaking through to new levels in heaven simply because God is infinite and we are finite. That means we will never come to the end of God. Paul reminds his readers, "No eye has seen, no ear has heard, and no mind has imagined what God has prepared for those who love him" (1 Corinthians 2:9).

The big picture

God has entrusted us with a magnificent world. Unfortunately in our fallenness, we have shredded large parts of that beautiful planet. We have also stained its soil with the blood of untold millions.

Instead of using our inborn genius to carefully direct and manage nature, we focus on stripping the earth for selfish advantage. Within a few years after Europeans met herds of thirty to sixty million bison in the American west, they were near extinction—most of them slaughtered for fun and left to rot. What kind of creature does that? And why? As we will see, the loftiness of humans created in God's image means that when severed from God they become by far more violent and dangerous than any other species on earth.

After we're done with the earth, it's going to require a complete renovation at the hands of our original creator.[1]

While we are still under obligation to manage nature well, other avenues of leadership have opened. God is pursuing a plan—the most important sequence of events in the history of the universe. This plan is introduced right here in Genesis, and we are in the middle of it all. Humans rescued by God have the fantastic opportunity to join into Jesus' work on earth.

The big picture

People without God, and many Christians too, feel the inner need for significance, but don't know what to do about it. People seek significance in money, power, fame, sexual conquest, or some type of uniqueness. But as Jesus observed, "what will it profit a man if he gains the whole world and forfeits his soul?" (Matthew 16:26). People who seek significance in the way of the world are left with a galling sense that there must be more.

Here is real significance: interactions that can change the course of eternal history!

---

[1] Randy Alcorn argues persuasively that the final state is not on a new or different planet, but a *renewed* planet—earth—fixed up and cleansed from the defilement of many centuries of abuse. Randy Alcorn, *Heaven* (Wheaton: Tyndale Momentum, 2004) Chapter 15.

11 Humans are Spiritual

Genesis 2:7

Genesis 2 describes the moment humans became spiritual beings.

> Then the Lord God formed man of dust from the ground, and breathed into his nostrils the breath of life; and man became a living being.
> (Genesis 2:7)

In Romans 1:19 we read, "That which is known about God is evident within people; for God made it evident to them." In other words, when you look "within," you should see something that makes God's existence and nature "evident" or obvious. What is this you see?—something humans have that no other animal has—a soul, or spirit.

What is a soul?

Genesis 2:7 says the man a living "being" or, according to the NASB margin, "literally, soul." The word here in Hebrew (*nephesh*) refers to the personal part of humans. Your mind, your feelings, and your will are key parts of your soul.[1]

The soul is non-material, and that's important. Humans have a material self, a body much like other animals, with a few major differences. But because your soul is non-material, it isn't subject to the mechanistic rules of physics. That's why you can reason freely, and therefore rationally. Your feelings and moral sense are real, not just chemical reactions. Apart from the existence of a non-material soul, you cannot be a real personal being.

---

[1] Like many Hebrew words, *nephesh* has a wide semantic range. It can refer to one's desire or one's life, and in that sense is also applied to animals. It's when applied to humans that it means "inner self."

"

Your soul survives the death of your body. Apart from a non-material soul, there would be no afterlife. That, in turn, would rob our present lives of ultimate meaning. All our lives would be building up to a point where we are nothing. And if you end up as nothing, you are nothing.

Most importantly, your soul or spirit gives you the ability to relate to God, and to be joined to his Spirit. Paul declares, "The one who joins himself to the Lord is one spirit with Him" (1 Corinthians 6:17).[2]

Separation of the soul from the body means physical death. When Rachael died in childbirth we read, "It came about as her soul was departing (for she died)..." (Genesis 35:1). Separation of your spirit from God means spiritual death.

Hebrews 12:9 calls God the "*Father of spirits.*" Apparently, God creates and implants an individual spirit into each human. It could happen at conception, or later, but definitely before birth, because, for instance, John the Baptist was filled with the Spirit in his mother's womb (Luke 1:15).

Validity of cumulative evidence

No single line of evidence will "prove" the existence of the soul. But multiple lines of evidence create a cumulative, weighty case. If you were a juror in a murder case, you would hear the prosecution build their case. Various lines of evidence usually bear on the question, resulting in a convincing case by the end.

---

[2] Interpreters debate whether humans are two part beings (body and soul) or three part beings (body, soul, and spirit). Three part interpreters point out that Paul says "may your spirit and soul and body be preserved complete" (1 Thessalonians 5:23). And the author of Hebrews says, "the word of God is living and active and sharper than any double-edged sword, piercing even to the point of dividing soul from spirit" (Hebrews 4:12). Under the three part view, your soul is your personality, and even non-believers have that. But the spirit is specifically for linking up with God. Until you receive God's Spirit, your own spirit is inert, or dead under this view (Ephesians 2:1). On the other hand, not all biblical authors follow this pattern, especially in the Old Testament, where humans are generally viewed as two-part beings. We will not take a position on this, but treat the spirit and soul as one and the same.

This is called "inference to the best explanation." Since we weren't there when the murder happened, the best we can do is follow the evidence to the most plausible explanation. In the case of criminal courts in our country, we add that the case must be "beyond reasonable doubt."

Note that it's beyond *reasonable doubt,* not beyond *any possible doubt.* People could choose to doubt anything. For instance, many people today doubt that the holocaust happened, or that we put a man on the moon. No amount of evidence makes any difference.

In the case of the existence and nature of the human soul, we have several key lines of evidence to consider:

- High order consciousness
- Self awareness
- Unique cognitive features:
    - Your mind's eye
    - Unbounded language
    - Creative aspect of language use
    - High order relations
    - Ability to freely analyze and draw conclusions
- Morality
- Near death experiences
- Other indications of free will
- Evidence of mind over matter
    - The placebo effect
    - Neuroplasticity
- Arguments from physics
- Discrediting parts of the no-soul view

High order consciousness

A good case can be made for mind-brain dualism, or substance dualism—that the human mind and brain are two different things. As we are using the word "mind" here, we mean high order thinking. Your high order mind is also your soul, your self. It uses your brain, but is free from the physical/chemical system involved in brain function.

Most secular proponents of the no-soul view focus exclusively on the most rudimentary aspects of consciousness—for instance, seeing the color green, or realizing you're in your bedroom when you wake up.

Yes, the term consciousness can be used in these ways, but that's not what we're discussing here. Animals have such rudimentary awareness of their surroundings, probably all the way down to light-sensitive microorganisms. So too, the ability to do simple learning, or to have feelings, do not necessarily signal high order consciousness and thought. Humans have something more.

Here are a handful of features found only in high order consciousness.

Self awareness

Your soul is your "self" or your mind. High order consciousness includes self-awareness. You can remember yourself as a child, even though every molecule in your body has changed since then. So you're not remembering the material "you." The "you" in there is your soul.

At the center is your awareness of yourself in history. That is, not that you dodge a stone someone throws at you, but that you can to review your life, relationships, accomplishments, reversals, and disasters. You can remember what happened, what you said, and how you felt at the time. As humans, we can ponder our past and what it means.

You can also see even your distant future, and lay plans to gain a good outcome. People go to college for years to prepare for a future career. Other animals aren't like this. They live in the moment. Any measures they take for the

future are short term and hardwired, like a spider spinning
exactly the same kind of web each time.

Unique cognitive features

Humans enjoy numerous whole categories of thought
unavailable to any other animal.

Second order thinking means you can think about your
thoughts. Pondering a train of thought could go on for days
or even years, and again, researchers have found no clear
evidence that other animals can ruminate or deliberate like
this over a problem.

Humans can think about *abstract things* like math,
relationships between cause and effect in a system, or what
is true. This kind of thinking transcends the tangible and
the material. Higher animals, like apes, can understand
visual relationships, like the blue balls versus green balls.
But they are unable to reason about non-tangible, abstract
things.

Humans understand *the concept of rules*—principles
generalized to apply in situations completely different than
the one in which the rule was learned—a crucial element in
the pathway to language.

Humans can form *general categories* based on structural
rather than perceptual criteria. For instance, at one point
my grandson acquired the concept of clocks. He began
pointing to different objects, whether a watch or a
grandfather clock, and pronouncing, "clock!" They didn't
look alike at all, but this two-year-old understood their
relationship in a way no nonhuman animal can.

Humans not only recognize when two physical objects are
perceptually similar, they can also recognize that two ideas,
two mental states, two grammatical constructions, or two

causal-logical relations are similar, again unlike any other animal.[3]

Your "mind's eye"

When we speak of the mind's eye, we are probably referring to the soul. You use your mind's eye to remember scenes from the past or to imagine scenes that never happened. You can project where a sequence of events is headed, imagining good or bad outcomes. You can even read a piece of fiction and envision the events described by another self.

Unbounded language

Another sign that you are spiritual comes from humans' elaborate use of language. True language is stimulus free, meaning you're not just crying out because someone stepped on your tail or invaded your territory. Human language can be about anything in any situation, and we don't need someone else to provoke it.

Real language must also be unbounded. A bird might sing, but you can identify birds by their songs. Most animals have only a tiny handful of vocalizations; one for anger, one for attracting a mate, one for warning, etc. Even a mocking bird, with over two hundred songs, is still limited to those songs.

That's nothing like human language. Using a handful of letters we can form a vast number of words, and by forming those words into sentences, we can create infinite meanings. We're all alone in having that capability.[4]

---

[3]For an excellent and honest research summary on these and other categories available only to humans see Derek C. Penn (UCLA), Keith J. Holyoak (UCLA), and Daniel J. Povinelli (U of L), "Darwin's mistake: Explaining the discontinuity between human and nonhuman minds," *Behavioral and Brain Sciences*, (2008) 109-178. This authoritative research survey is available free online.

[4] The argument that whales or dolphins might be speaking advanced languages fails. With all the extensive study in recent years, and all the sophisticated decoding techniques we have, we surely would have decoded these languages by now. What we find is similar to other animals, with a limited number of signals and no syntax.

Creative aspect of language use

Mark Baker, an expert in linguistics, gives us some amazing observations based on current neurological-linguistic studies. He points out that Noam Chomsky, father of modern linguistics, defined three components to the human language faculty:

> 1. The *lexicon,* or list of words, could be compared to the building materials assembled to build a building, like concrete, steel, wood, etc.

> 2. The *grammar* or *syntax* is a set of rules for combining words. So, "I threw the ball at him" is different than "He threw the ball at me," even though using the same word stems. The slight changes in spelling (like "him" versus "he," and word position in the sentence completely change the meaning. In our analogy, this would be the skilled workmen who know how to build with steel, bricks, wood or whatever.

> 3. And finally what Chomsky came to call the "Creative Aspect of Language Use," or *CALU.* In our analogy, the workers are there, the materials are there, but what are they to build? They need an architect and manager to select materials and tell the workmen what to build with the materials.[5]

The human creative aspect can select and modify words, and then assemble them into actual sentences—with correct word order, case, tense, mood, gender, etc.—on the fly, with blinding speed, and with little effort. Baker points out that nothing like this creative aspect is found in any other animal.[6]

---

[5] Mark Baker "Brains and Souls; Grammar and Speaking" in Mark Baker and Stewart Goetz Ed. *The Soul Hypothesis: Investigations into the Existence of the Soul* (NY: Continuum, 2010), 77.

[6] Anderson says no animal has ever grasped even number 2—syntax—in spite of decades of training various apes. Stephen Anderson, *Dr Dolittle's Delusion: Animals and the Uniqueness of Human Language,* (Newhaven, Yale University Press, 2004) 297. He also unmasks the duplicity of some who make extravagant

Here's the most fascinating part: After 140 years of research into how different regions of the brain contribute to vocabulary and syntax, neuroscientists have learned a great deal about which tissues in the brain are responsible for Chomsky's first two components—vocabulary and syntax. However, they have learned "almost nothing" about the location for the CALU, or creative aspect.

Dr. Baker observes, "The CALU seems not to be directly dependent on the brain in the way that many other interacting functions (like vocabulary and grammar) are." Instead, he thinks, "We are justified to think that the CALU is a function of the soul more than the body."[7]

This is an astonishing and persuasive, physical argument for the existence of the soul.

High order relations

Humans alone are capable of comprehending high order relations. Penn states,

> "By the age of 3, all normal humans are able to reason about the higher-order relation between small-scale artificial spatial models and large-scale spatial relations in the real world (maps, diagrams, gestures, etc.).[8]

In other words, a child can understand that a diagram of a volcano stands for any volcano, not just "the" volcano. They can follow a map to a destination. No other animal will ever achieve that.

---

claims for "talking apes." He exposes their faking, lying, and refusal to share their data or videos. Some naturalistic and animal rights advocates are desperate to show that humans and animals are almost the same, but without success.

[7] Mark Baker, "Brains and Souls," in *The Soul Hypothesis*, 81.

[8] Derek Penn, et al. "Darwin's Mistake," 114. A critic replies, "Kudos to Penn et al. for admitting what, if it were not politically incorrect (somewhere between Holocaust denial and rejection of global warming), would be obvious to all: the massive cognitive discontinuity between humans and all other animals." Derek Bickerton, "Darwin's last word: How words changed cognition," *Behavioral and Brain Sciences*, (2008) 31:2.

When reading no-soul critics, you will find that most are completely mired in the details of how neurons and connections in the brain work. But while such research is important for a number of reasons, none of the minutiae really contributes to our understanding of the larger picture—high order consciousness, the mind, or the soul.

They are like a research team that studies a Tolkien novel. They report back on the properties of the ink, glue, and paper, breaking down the complete molecular makeup of the piece. Have they explained it? Not at all. They have completely missed the main point. It's a story! It has characters and events drawn out of imagination. This is no different than modern no-soul researchers' fixation on neurological details, but looking right past high order consciousness.

Ability to freely analyze and draw conclusions

If we weren't able to freely analyze, sift, and appraise information before reaching a conclusion, we wouldn't really be thinking our way to a conclusion. Instead, we would be driven by the chemistry and physics in our brain, not by the thing known—the truth.

Weighing alternatives, judging the relative validity of arguments—these require unfettered freedom. But no-soul thinkers can't explain how molecules and electrical current could result in freedom. That's why most neuroscientists say freedom is an illusion.

Consider lions. They stand high in the hierarchy of intelligence among animals. They're social, they engage in group hunting and ambush—pretty advanced. But every year, they watch a million wildebeests strike off on their thousand mile migration. Why don't the lions follow them as a secure source of food? They can't. They're territorial. Every year some of the lions will die of starvation during the wildebeest's absence, but they can't adapt.

This highlights the difference between animal and human intelligence. Animal thought is stiff and usually predictable—exactly what you would expect from thinking that is limited to a physical brain. Human thinking is free and unbounded.

Humans are so adaptable and flexible that they have populated every ecosphere on earth—polar regions, swamps, deserts, mountains, valleys, and islands. Meanwhile, the second most intelligent species on earth—chimpanzees—are endangered, because they can't adapt to the loss of habitat.[9]

Again, mental determinism and boundedness like this fits with a physical view of the brain and mind. But while physicalism fits chimps and lions, it will not fit humans.

The creativity in human behavior doesn't seem determined. As Penn observes, "The functional discontinuity between human and nonhuman minds pervades nearly every domain of cognition."[10]

Consider this watch (chosen because it's easier to see the mechanism than is a computer, but really no different). The wheels and notches fit into one another in a rigid and fixed way.

When one wheel turns, the others turn with it.

It doesn't know what it's doing. It doesn't know anything. It isn't thinking. It can't reason. It's just a machine. It does what it's designed to do—tell time.

How could freedom emerge from such a system? It can't. And neurons, neurochemicals, and electrical current make

---

[9] I drew this from Michael Gazzaniga, *Who's in Charge? Free will and the science of the brain,* (NY: Harper Collins Publishing: 2011) 9.

[10] Derek Penn et al. "Darwin's Mistake: Explaining the discontinuity between human and nonhuman minds," *Behavioral and Brain Sciences,* (2008) 31, 109.

up a physical machine more complex, but not really no different. These don't choose how to react. Their reaction depends on physics and chemistry. That's why most neuroscientists simply deny that freedom exists, in spite of the fact that humans' thinking (including the scientists' own thinking) would be invalid and pointless apart from real freedom.

Real freedom does exist, and it comes to us because God introduced a non-material soul into each human.

C. S. Lewis explains:

> For [the theist], the human mind in the act of knowing is set free, in the measure required, from the huge nexus of non-rational causation; free from this to be determined by the truth known.[11]

Doug Groothuis puts it another way:

> When we reason from a premise to a conclusion, we are not thinking in terms of material causes but rather in terms of rational inference.[12]

Correct. But the laws of rationality are different than the laws of physics. Rational inference has nothing to do with how physical entities interact with each other. Our minds analyze and evaluate external things—the conclusions are not "caused" by those things.

You can see the success of reason in, for instance, advanced technology like that in your phone. The device's amazing capabilities were all created as inventions at one time or another. So, investigation and reasoning must be accurately understanding and reshaping the material world. Otherwise the complex device wouldn't work. That points to free will, including intent (not just freedom in the sense of randomness).

---

[11] C. S. Lewis, *Miracles* (London: Macmillan, 1947) 47.

[12] Douglas Groothuis, *Christian Apologetics: A Comprehensive Case for Biblical Faith* (Wheaton: IVP Academic, 2011) Kindle electronic edition Location 4406.

Intent and freedom of thought lead, in turn, to existence of the soul. Who or what is intending and analyzing? Not the matter in your brain. Your mind may use your brain but something must lie behind the chemicals and electrical impulses making up brain activity in order to have intention and freedom. Matter by itself cannot have an intention or freedom.

Morality

Another indication that we have souls comes from our moral sense. Everyone knows that animals are incapable of moral or immoral behaviors. They lack the high order consciousness needed to make morally responsible choices. Only humans are capable of racism, hate, or theft. When a dog "steals" some food from another dog, he's just being a dog. The ability to be moral or immoral comes directly from our souls.

Near death experiences?

A growing number of cases, now numbering in the thousands, involve people coming near to death, usually on an operating table or hospital bed, only to suddenly see themselves from outside their own body. The number of cases is increasing rapidly, because of advances in our ability to bring people back from the edge of death.

These events have typically been dismissed as hallucinations or dreams, but that's changing. The main reason for change is that many of these victims come back recounting things they saw happening in the operating room while they were technically dead, and usually under general anesthesia.

Anyone who has experienced general anesthesia knows there's no dreaming or hallucinating. The last thing you remember is the breathing mask coming down. Next thing you know, you're in the recovery room. Besides, how would a dream enable someone to recount in detail, conversations and actions going on in the operating room while he or she was out cold?

If you're not familiar with these cases, the best thing to do is read the available literature and watch some of the fascinating videos on YouTube.[13]

Other signs of mind over matter

The mind and the brain are not the same thing, even though they work together. We noted earlier that under "substance dualism" the brain can affect the mind, but the mind can also affect the brain.

Consider some things that don't fit the no-soul view.

The placebo effect

Since the 1970's new drugs must be tested and shown more effective than fake pills, or "placebos," given to a control group. The placebo has a significant, measurable healing effect. But the patient is not taking any drug. Rather, his or her mind is doing the healing.

The placebo effect should not be confused with natural healing processes. It depends exclusively on what a patient *believes*. Materialist neuroscience has long regarded the placebo effect as a problem, but it's one of the best attested phenomena in medicine.[14]

The placebo effect varies depending on the condition being treated, and from one patient to another. But the fact that it is measurable and significant (sometimes helping up to 40% of patients tested) points to a clear case of non-material mind over matter. It's not a mechanical

---

[13]Raymond Moody, *Life After Life: The Bestselling Original Investigation That Revealed "Near-Death Experiences,* has been updated (NY: HarperOne, 2015). One remarkable case involves a woman born blind, but could see for the first time during her near death experience. Also interesting is Jeffrey Long, MD. *Evidence of the Afterlife: The Science of Near Death Experiences,* (NY: HarperOne, 2011). https://www.youtube.com/watch?v=gKyQJDZuMHE. I don't necessarily subscribe to the religious interpretations these and other authors offer, but the data is provocative.

[14] Mark Baker and Stewart Goetz: *The Soul Hypothesis*, 14.

transmission of molecules or energy. It's what one believes—a state of mind—that causes real changes in the body. That's why it is only found in humans. You have to be able to believe something.

Neuroscientist, Mario Beauregard says,

> Neuroimaging studies have now demonstrated that the placebo effect is real. It is not simply an artifact of medical record keeping or folklore. But when we try to understand how it works, we must look not only at the brain but also at the mind.[15]

In 2005, *New Scientist* ran an article about "13 Things That Don't Make Sense." The placebo effect was number one on the list. But it only makes no sense if you believe the mind doesn't exist or is powerless.

The placebo effect is not merely patients mistakenly reporting improvement. Studies show that when Parkinson's patients' tremors declined under placebo effect, their brains also decreased activity in the related area, as shown on PET scans.[16]

Neuroplasticity

The emerging science of functional MRI and PET scans has unveiled hitherto unknown properties of the brain.

Beauregard explains:

> A central dogma of early neuroscience was that the neurons of the adult brain do not change. However, modern neuroscience now recognizes that the brain can reorganize (this reorganization is called "neuroplasticity") throughout life, not only in early childhood.[17]

---

[15] Mario Beauregard and Denyse O'Leary, *The Spiritual Brain: A Neuroscientist's Case for the Existence of the Soul,* (HarperOne; Reprint edition, 2008) 60.

[16] R. de la Fuente-Fernandez et al., "Expectation and Dopamine Release: Mechanism of the Placebo Effect in Parkinson's Disease," *Science* 293 (2001): 1164-66.

[17] Mario Beauregard, *The Spiritual Brain,* 118.

In learning about neuroplasticity, science is disclosing that, rather than the brain controlling and creating the illusion of mind, it's actually the mind that can shape the brain.

Jeffrey Schwartz, a nonmaterialist UCLA neuropsychiatrist, treats obsessive-compulsive disorder—a neuropsychiatric disease marked by distressing, intrusive, and unwanted thoughts—by getting patients to reprogram their brains.

Their minds change their brains. When an unwanted thought or urge strikes, they simply repeat a short series of true statements. Within weeks, brain scans show visible, measurable changes in the areas of the brain involved in those compulsions. The patients report remarkable freedom.

In one example scientists were able to guide spider phobic patients to re-program their brains to the point where they could hold and pet tarantula spiders!

This is nothing less than 'mind over matter.'[18] The materialistic no-soul position doesn't fit this picture at all.

Discrediting parts of the no-soul view

How good are the arguments for physicalism (the belief that humans have no soul and are nothing but matter)? They are weak or nonexistent. For several reasons, these claims lack credibility.

Claiming they know what they cannot know

Any view claiming that all our most basic perceptions are illusions bears an incredible burden of proof. This burden would be just as heavy as convincing me that what my eyes see or what my ears here are all illusion. I don't need to prove that what I perceive is real. *They* have to prove that it's not real.

Thomas Nagel is an atheistic professor, but agrees with this view. In his review of Daniel Dennet's recent book arguing

---

[18] Mario Beuregard, *The Spiritual Brain*, 13.

that consciousness, free will, and the self are all illusions, he wrote,

> I am reminded of the Marx Brothers line: "Who are you going to believe, me or your own eyes?" Dennett asks us to turn our backs on what is glaringly obvious—that in consciousness we are immediately aware of real subjective experiences.[19]

Think about it. If we can't trust our own senses, we have no way to know anything! If I'm that deceived about my high order consciousness, about my freedom to choose what I want, or that I'm a moral being, why trust any conclusion I arrive at? Why trust any conclusion Dennet reaches?

So how do the no-soul apologists perform on bearing such a heavy burden? Poorly! In fact, no-soul thinkers offer almost nothing in favor of their view. Their biggest argument is that the existence of a soul hasn't been proven. But of course, their view hasn't been proven either, and in fact, no worldview can be proven in the mathematical sense. On the other hand, the evidence for the soul is good. Evidence against the soul's existence is weak to nonexistent.

So naturalists frame the discussion, saying, "You have to prove everything, we don't have to prove anything." That guarantees the conclusion will always come out in favor of naturalism, not because naturalism is true, but because of special pleading (the fallacy of putting your opponent under rules you don't follow yourself).

Naturalists only make rudimentary observations about brain function and for the most part dismiss belief in a soul as absurd and primitive. "No one believes in that anymore," they sputter, as though that makes their position true. And yet the claim is false, because the vast majority of people do believe in the soul now, and throughout history.

---

[19] Thomas Nagel, "Is Consciousness an Illusion?" *New York Review of Books,* Mar. 9, 2017.

No-soul believers base a lot of their case on the fact that when people get brain injuries in one or another part of the brain, it changes their personalities. The assumption is that, because we can show linkage between parts of the brain and given behaviors or states of mind, that shows that the brain is all there is. The idea of a distinct "mind" is unwarranted, they claim. But these observations really don't carry much weight.

Theists argue that the mind works through and with the brain in a way similar to someone driving a car. Imagine driving and suddenly blowing out one of your front tires (a brain injury). That car isn't going to drive the same. If two tires on the same side blew out, the car would be lurching and weaving down the street in a very broken way. It doesn't mean there's no driver in the car. Or that the tires are the driver. Yet that's essentially what no-soul, no-mind thinkers argue.

Of course, if the engine blew up, you couldn't drive at all. That still wouldn't mean the car has no driver. It would mean the driver has no outlet.

When did science discover that the self is an illusion? That must have been an incredible discovery! No. There was no discovery; just dogmatic claims with no backing. The discoveries have been pointing the other direction.

When you meet people, you don't learn about them by studying their bodies or their brains. You learn about people by finding out how they feel, what they think, their history, what they're passionate about, what their worldview is…. That's because people aren't what their brains are, they are what their souls are.

Necessarily God?

Some wonder, does the existence of a soul necessarily require the existence of God? Yes, it does! The soul must be non-material in order to have its characteristic freedom, as we've seen. But no physical process (like evolution) could ever create something non-material. If humans have souls, then the creator God is real, and that's a fact well understood by no-soul apologists.

Thomas Nagel, again, an atheistic professor of philosophy admits, "Consciousness is the most conspicuous obstacle to a comprehensive naturalism that relies only on the resources of physical science.[20] His honesty is commendable. Few others are so honest.

The big picture

All common sense evidence, scientific findings, and our own intuitive sense point one direction—God's word is truth. We are truly people created in God's image. Our non-material souls are real. They will survive the death of our bodies. And they enable us to relate directly with God.

---

[20] Thomas Nagel, *Mind and Cosmos: Why the Materialist Neodarwinian Conception of Nature Is Almost Certainly False,* (Oxford University Press, 2012) 35.

12 Humans Accomplish
Genesis 2:15

> Then the Lord God took the man and put him into the Garden of Eden to cultivate it and keep it. (Genesis 2:15)

Eden was apparently a vast area encompassing the entire Fertile Crescent and Arabian Desert. The Garden of Eden was "to the east" (v. 8) within that larger area. "The land" mentioned several times in this section, probably refers to this area, not to the whole earth. The Hebrew word *eretz* can mean either the whole world or a more limited area. For instance, "*eretz* Israel" is the land of Israel.

The statement that, "God had not yet sent rain to water the earth," (v. 5) could be understood the same way—he had not sent rain on this limited area since the recreation in chapter 1. Or, he had not sent rain since planting the garden.

Work

God didn't put Adam into the garden merely to enjoy it. He was also to cultivate it and keep it. Here we have another characteristic of humans before the fall—the need to work. Humans are made to accomplish something.

God's plan for humans includes some rest, as seen in the Sabbath law. But just laying around too much, enjoying the surroundings, playing video games, or being entertained, is sub-human. No wonder that way of life leads to depression and apathy.

Lazy people are violating their own nature by laying around too much. At the same time, their depressed sense of pointlessness makes it even harder to get up off the couch and go forward to accomplish something.

Those who deny this human attribute are severely censured in the book of Proverbs under the term "sluggards." The sluggard is more intent on cultivating personal comfort and avoiding exertion than on accomplishing anything. Here are a few.

> The soul of the sluggard craves and gets nothing,
> But the soul of the diligent is made fat. (Proverbs 13:4).

In other words, living as a sluggard is a life of selfish lust.

> The sluggard does not plow after the autumn, So he begs during the harvest and has nothing." (Proverbs 20:4)

This proverb calls our attention to the selfishness of the sluggard. He sees nothing wrong with being a burden to others. He's a love-taker.

> The desire of the sluggard puts him to death, For his hands refuse to work; All day long he is craving, While the righteous gives and does not hold back. (Proverbs 21:25-26)

Here again, the selfish, lustful fantasy life of the sluggard leaves him empty handed, while the "righteous" or godly one gains happiness from what he can give out.

Such a person has grasped one of the key reasons for working—as Paul explains: "He who steals must steal no longer; but rather he must labor, performing with his own hands what is good, *so that he will have something to share with one who has need*" (Ephesians 4:28 emphasis added).

The lazy way of life is such a serious sin that the New Testament calls for the most extreme form of church discipline—removal from fellowship—for those who continue in it (2 Thessalonians 3:12-14).

At the same time, Paul commends the goal-oriented life: "Do you not know that those who run in a race all run, but only one receives the prize? Run in such a way that you may win" (1 Corinthians 9:24). And here, in context, he has in view excelling in ministry.

God works

Our interior design, including our need to accomplish something meaningful, is based on God's own nature as a worker. Jesus said to his accusers, "My Father is working until now, and I myself am working" (John 5:17). That made his enemies so mad they sought to kill him.

But what he said was true. God is a worker. He is accomplishing important tasks. Jesus also said, "Behold, I cast out demons and perform cures today and tomorrow, and the third day I reach My goal" (Luke 13:32). Jesus was goal-directed during his whole life.

God lays plans and achieves them. To Israel God said, "I know the plans I have for you... plans to prosper you and not to harm you, plans to give you a hope and a future" (Jeremiah 29:11).

So, considering that we are created in the image of God, we should not shy away from devoting ourselves to working and accomplishing. The most important accomplishments are those with eternal significance. Paul says, "For we are his workmanship, created in Christ Jesus for good works, which God prepared beforehand, that we should walk in them" (Ephesians 2:10).

He also makes clear that God's goal has now been entrusted to us: "God was in Christ reconciling the world to Himself, not counting their trespasses against them, and He has committed to us the word of reconciliation" (2 Corinthians 5:19). So every believer gets to take part in furthering God's program and plan that began right here in Genesis.

Heaven

The picture of us in heaven, floating in the clouds playing a harp, comes from Satan. Can you imagine your fifty thousandth year strumming a harp? Instead, we can anticipate agriculture (beating your swords into plowshares, Micah 4:3-4) the arts (music, Revelation 5:9) learning (imagine hearing that Jesus is holding a seminar Thursday on how he came up with the DNA system!).

God is going to be right there, accessible to us. We will be going deeper and deeper into our relationship with God and our knowledge of him. Because God is infinite we can rest assured that that heaven will never be boring. No matter how far we progress there will always be more to learn and enjoy.

Regained

People without God have problems with work. Many view work as a place to base their identity, or sense of importance. The result is that they are looking to their career for something it can never deliver. What does the world say to do if you're working your career, but not feeling a rewarding sense of identity anymore? Work harder! Climb higher!

For others, work is nothing but a boring way to put food on the table. The boss is a fool, the shop is dysfunctional, I hate getting up each day...." Even some Christians point to the thorns and thistles that make work burdensome and irksome. But that was *after* the fall. From this verse we see that our desire and need to work were part of humans before they fell from God's will.

The big picture

God gave us work to do for our own good. You need to learn to enjoy working and accomplishing worthwhile tasks. Don't value your work life for fallen reasons, like pride or a weak sense of identity.

Instead, view your work life as a creative outlet and as meeting important needs. Walking followers should learn to enjoy the act of going out to work, whether it's for needed income, or as a worker for God. It becomes especially enjoyable when the Holy Spirit moves through you for positive impact on your world.

This verse is an important underlying basis for the concept of "every member ministry." New Testament teaching makes it clear that serving and doing ministry is the birthright of every child of God. Paul's expression, "But to each one is given the manifestation of the Spirit for the common good" (1 Corinthians 12:7) means "to each and every one is given...." In Ephesians 4 he writes that growth and health in the body of Christ depend on "what every joint supplies, according to the proper working of each individual part" (v. 16).

The big picture

Believers should acquire a good career where they can work to bear fruit in terms of income, and also enjoy being a good, competent worker. We don't see our careers as defining us or as a means to get rich. Followers of Jesus should be more interested in making a difference through their giving.

In the body of Christ we not only have regular opportunities to serve, but we learn the deeper joy of serving *together*. Working as a team to serve the Lord, win people to the gospel, and build up fellow believers is downright fun and rewarding. Believers serving in community together are right down the center of what God made us to be.

13 Humans Have Free Will
Genesis 2:9; 16-17

> Out of the ground the Lord God caused to grow every tree that is pleasing to the sight and good for food; the tree of life also in the midst of the garden, and the tree of the knowledge of good and evil.
>
> And the Lord God commanded the man, saying, "From any tree of the garden you may eat freely; but from the tree of the knowledge of good and evil you shall not eat, for in the day that you eat from it you shall surely die." (Genesis 2: 9, 16-17)

Verse 9 reveals that God created two important trees in the Garden of Eden, called the "tree of life," and "the tree of the knowledge of good and evil." We will examine the trees' names below.

God created an environment that met humans' needs. But he also introduced something that had nothing to do with biological need—a tree bearing forbidden fruit. Why was this tree's fruit forbidden? Because God said so.

Why two trees?

Why would God do that? The answer points again to the nature of humans created in the image of God. They are moral beings. Humans are so lofty that they can seek and enjoy a relationship with God himself. And that loftiness means that just as they can choose to relate to God and follow him, they can choose to turn away from him.

People created in God's image have free will, and that's essential if they are to be capable of moral behavior. An organism that cannot choose what it does cannot be moral.

It's an animal. It's doing what its environment and architecture dictate.

Why chide troupes of chimpanzees for waging war with each other, as they occasionally do? Why not prosecute and imprison those who kill one of their own? Because it's not immoral. Chimps killing each other might be something we hate to see, but it's part of being a chimp.

Humans are different, as this passage reveals. Because they are imbued with a soul, they are not conditioned to do what they do; they choose what to do (especially true before the fall). Having the power of choice also opens the door to the most positive ability we have—the ability to love.

God puts massive importance on love. He is so in to love that the apostle John can say,

> Beloved, let us love one another, for love is from God; and everyone who loves is born of God and knows God. The one who does not love does not know God, for God is love. (1 John 4:7-8)

The statement, "God is love" is hyperbole—deliberate exaggeration for effect. God is more than love. But it signals God's true values system. What does God think is important? The answer comes back throughout the Bible—love.

But in order to love, especially at the high level of God's love, free will is essential. Imagine recording a voice on your phone saying, "I love you! You're awesome. I love hanging out with you," and so on. Then, you could pull your phone out and play it whenever you feel lonely. Absurd? Yes, because this isn't love. It's just saying what you programmed it to say. Real love has to be freely chosen by a high order being.

So God provided the first humans the opportunity to choose. The most important choice they would ever make was whether to trust and follow God, or turn away from him and strike out on their own. The two trees stood for that choice.

Free choosing creatures are capable of the highest good. But they are also, by definition, capable of extreme evil choices. That capability has resulted in human history as we know it—wars, atrocities, and all. Once people were separate from God and going their own way, anything was possible. No atrocity was so bad that fallen beings couldn't commit it.

We conclude that, by nature, freedom entails the best or the worst outcomes.

God looked at the possible negatives compared to the possible positives under freedom and decided it was worth it. He created free-will creatures. We have no way to evaluate that decision beyond saying that God made it. We don't know what factors led to his choice, but those of us who follow him trust that it was the right decision.

Critics claim God was himself evil because he created a situation where evil could break out and flourish. They point out that God knew the negative choice was coming, and that's true.[1] But God only created the *possibility* of evil. Humans created the *actuality* of evil.

---

[1] Ephesians 1:4 unambiguously declares that the omniscient God knew creation would lead to the fall of humans, and the resulting need for his plan of rescue trough Jesus. People wonder, how could freedom be real if God knows the future infallibly? We don't know how, but scripture is clear that human freedom and divine omniscience do co-exist. Openness theologians err when they suggest that God doesn't know what free choosing beings will choose. He does, and that's the clear teaching of scripture.

Hyper-Calvinists also err when they claim that God knows the future because he makes things come out a certain way. That's true in some key cases, but not in all (compare Ezekiel 38:4 with Acts 14:16).

We don't need to explain how God knows the future in spite of our real freedom and we never could explain it. We aren't omniscient and could probably never understand what it's like. Much about God lies beyond our comprehension "The secret things belong to the Lord our God, but the things revealed belong to us and to our sons forever..." (Deuteronomy 29:29).

It could be some kind of extra-dimensional thing that allows him to see outside of time. After all, if Einstein is right, both time and space are a continuum and both came into being at the big bang. So, if God is the creator, he must exist outside that continuum. At the same time he can enter into it, as he did in Christ. For good discussion of the need for compatibilism (that both divine sovereignty and

Others argue that God should have created people who had free will but always choose good, not evil. This is a plain contradiction in terms, leading to absurdity. Any version of freedom that can only make one choice is double talk. That's why God provided the forbidden fruit. Adam had the option of going with God or going against him.

As with previous attributes of humans created in God's image, this one fits the pattern we've seen.

God is moral

Postmodern people find it difficult to understand that God is a moral being. To postmodern culture, morality is nothing but personal preference, or at most, a cultural construct. But God's nature is not a preference or a construct. He is eternal and unchanging good. All true moral norms are based on what God is, on his character.

God doesn't decide or decree what is good or evil. Rather, his character is what it is, and that is the basis for all good and evil in the universe. As the creator and owner of the universe he has the right to reveal moral norms based on his own character that other, responsible moral beings should follow. God's goodness also means he can be counted on to always do the best thing for his creatures.

God is also free. He does whatever he chooses, consistent with his own character. Since God is truthful, "it is impossible for God to lie," (Hebrews 6:18). And this is true of all his attributes. However, we should never develop theological teachings that suggest God has to do this or that.

Freedom in heaven

Because of the undeniable link between love relationships and free will, we can safely predict that even in the eternal state, we will remain free choosing beings. Yet, we can also

---

free will are compatible) see D. A. Carson, *The Difficult Doctrine of the Love of God,* (Wheaton: Crossway Books, 2000) 50-53.

safely predict that the future state will never again experience a moral fall from God's will. This conclusion is based on the "once and for all time" statements in Hebrews (e.g. Hebrews 7:27; 9:12; 25-26;10:10) as well as Revelation 21:4:

> He will wipe away every tear from their eyes; and there will no longer be any death; there will no longer be any mourning, or crying, or pain; the first things have passed away.

How is this possible? How can people, or other creatures, be free, and yet never again rebel against God? Earlier we suggested that's absurd. So what's the difference?

One difference will be our experience. Several passages indicate that the present revolt and its horrific consequences will be a big part of the reason people in heaven will have no desire for evil. Unlike Adam and Eve, humans in the world to come will remember their personal experience with evil. Other creatures who aren't a part of our experience on Earth have watched and learned from it as well (Ephesians 2:7; 3:10; Colossians 2:15; 1 Peter 1:12). But we are the only ones to actually experience it.

People who remember the horrors of a fallen world will never want to return to that again. Also, we will no longer have sin natures that cause us to desire sin.

Of course, it won't hurt that Satan and other anti-God forces won't be around anymore.

Freedom regained

Free will can be damaged. When people fall into sin, they can lose a significant part of their free will. This is what Jesus meant when he said that "everyone who commits sin is the slave of sin" (John 8:34).

In fact, fallen people have so lost their freedom when it comes to following God, that nothing less than a miraculous intervention by the Holy Spirit can enable them to believe and follow Jesus (John 6:44). Fortunately, Jesus promised to draw all men to himself (John. 12:32). But we can still say no.

Once people receive the new birth, everything changes. In our new position in Christ, we have the basis for deliverance from slavery to sin. Paul explains:

> Our old self was crucified with Him, in order that our body of sin might be done away with, so that we would no longer be slaves to sin; for he who has died is freed from sin. (Romans 6:6-7)

By presenting ourselves to God through faith as those alive from the dead, we release the power of the Holy Spirit to begin restoring our freedom. But it's a growth process. This isn't describing a sudden deliverance. It assumes that we walk according the Spirit, taking full advantage of the means of growth available to us, like God's word, Christian fellowship, and prayer.

The big picture

Because people are moral beings, true moral guilt becomes a reality. To say that someone is guilty doesn't refer to a feeling of guilt. We all know what it's like to feel guilty. But the feeling of guilt is only an imperfect artifact of true moral guilt.

Sometimes people feel guilty for things that aren't their fault or for things that aren't wrong at all. At other times people fail to feel any guilt, even though they are quite guilty. So guilt feelings are subjective and unreliable. True guilt is not a feeling; it's a willful violation of God's moral character.

As we move into the third chapter in Genesis, we will see the awful devastation wrought by negative moral choice—now known by the S word—sin.

14 Humans are Relational

Genesis 2:18-20

> Then the Lord God said, "It is not good for the man to be alone; I will make him a helper corresponding to him." (Genesis 2:18)

During the earlier days of creation in Chapter 1, we see a refrain:

and God saw that the light was good (v. 4)
and God saw that it was good (v. 10)
and God saw that it was good. (v. 12)
and God saw that it was good (v. 18)
and God saw that it was good. (v. 21)
and God saw that it was good. (v. 25)
God saw all that He had made, and behold, it was very good. (v. 31)

This last strengthened form came after he created Adam on day 6. Now we hear something different: God said, "It is not good for the man to be alone" (2:18). Something is wrong. Adam is incomplete, defective. He's alone.

God's solution is "I will make him a helper[1] suitable [NASB margin = "lit. corresponding to"] for him." This is suitability in the sense of someone who has the same nature he has—a living soul, created in God's image.

In the next verses in Genesis, vs. 19-20, God brought the animals to Adam so he could name them. Animals are so cool; this must have been a blast for Adam. But as the text hinted already, God was really giving Adam an object

---

[1] Modern critics like to claim that calling woman a "helper" is a gateway into patriarchy and a low view of women. They fail to understand the Hebrew concept of serving love. God calls himself a helper of the people, and he certainly is not inferior (e.g. Psalm 10:14; 30:10; 54:4).

lesson. As sweet as the animals were, the verdict remained: "but for Adam there was not found a helper corresponding to him" (v. 20).

Yes, we can love like animals do—simple affection, like you might feel with your dog or cat. But especially with fellow believers, we can take love to a new level.

For humans, relationship is not secondary or ancillary. We are relational at our core. Our deepest need isn't for food, sex, glory, or wealth. Our deepest need is for love. That's why we need those who "correspond to" us with whom we can develop relationships.

Anthropologists like to say that humans are social. So are other species. Humans are way more. We don't often get to see this attribute fully displayed, because humanity's fall away from God has severely damaged our ability to relate successfully. That's why people try to substitute other things for love.

God is relational

Humans are so selfish they find it very difficult to fully believe in the love of God. Even believers have to gradually discover over a period of years how deep his love is. But that's the key to our own growth. John says, "We have come to know and have believed the love which God has for us" (1 John 4:16). And "We love because he first loved us" (v. 19).

Relationships in heaven

Why will we never be bored in heaven? Because heaven is going to be a place of love. Eden was the forerunner of the New Earth we will enjoy forever. But even there, when God in close relationship with Adam, he said "it is not good for man to be alone." In God's design, more is needed.

Calvin was wrong when he said, "To be in Paradise and live with God is not to speak to each other and be heard by each other, but is only to enjoy God, to feel his good will, and rest in him."[2]

You see the correct view from Paul, who reminds the Thessalonians of their relationship with him, "We loved you so much" (1 Thessalonians 2:8). And then follows with the thought, "What is our hope, our joy, or the crown in which we will glory in the presence of our Lord Jesus when he comes? Is it not you? Indeed, you are our glory and joy" (1 Thessalonians 2:19-20). You can see how Paul was eagerly looking forward to continuing their relationship in heaven.

Passages about heaven make clear that there will be cities and people coming together to rejoice at feasts (Revelation 21:10; Isaiah 25:6; 61:4). David knew that with his dead infant son, "I will go to him, but he will not return to me" (2 Samuel 12:23). The relational component in humans is part of God's permanent and good design.

Regaining our relational component

If you move deeper into the love of God, you can take what you learn and apply it in community with God's people. Believers building love relationships with each other are able to take love to a new level. Paul talks about believers "speaking the truth in love... so that the whole body [i.e. Christian community] is healthy and growing and full of love" (Ephesians 4:15-16).

When they asked Jesus what the greatest commandment was, he answered that loving God was first. But he wasn't willing to leave it at that. Instead, he went on, "A second is equally important: 'Love your neighbor as yourself.'" (Matthew 22:39).

So according to Jesus, loving God cannot be separated from loving fellow humans. Whether it's the people of God, the family, or non-Christians, this is a huge goal for walking

---

[2] Cited in Randy Alcorn, *Heaven* (Wheaton: Tyndale House Publishers, 2003) Kindle version, Location 5758.

believers. Everywhere else we turn, the same message comes across—love relationships are not just good, they stand at the center of everything that's important.

Believers who grow spiritually can be healed so much that even successful marriages become possible.

The big picture

Whenever humans try to get by on materialism, glory, or sensuality instead of love, God says, "It is not good." The path to success in love begins when we meet Jesus. Then, it includes discovering every area of selfishness, unwillingness to forgive, bitterness, and ingratitude—things the Holy Spirit reveals when you're actively building into your family and Christian community.

If we stick together and continue to invest in our relationships in the community of God's people and elsewhere, God will teach us how to fully reclaim our wonderful relational attribute.

15 Humans are Creative

Genesis 2:19

Naming the animals

> And out of the ground the Lord God formed every beast of the field and every bird of the sky, and brought them to the man to see what he would call them; and whatever the man called a living creature, that was its name. (Genesis 2:19)

Earlier, we saw that this naming of the animals was intended to teach Adam the difference between him and the other animals. But here we consider another aspect of the naming. It's an unmistakable mark of the soul—creativity.

Where does Adam get the names he assigns to the animals? He creates them out of thin air. That's human. Unlike non-human animals, humans can freely and easily compose novel things in great profusion—a key pathway to language.[1]

---

[1] Anderson, a professor of linguistics at Yale, observes, "The power of human language derives from our ability to use it to say (and understand) things that are novel. If the set of messages were limited and fixed in advance, this possibility would not exist. (e.g., bee language)." In bee language, the bee's abdomen wobbles a certain number of times as the bee walks in a certain direction, corresponding to the location of a nectar find. It's all very fixed and predictable, unlike human language.

He also surveys research claiming apes learned to talk using sign language. "All of these gestural activities on the part of primates are... simply an inventory of some relatively limited, finite number of discrete messages.... We have no evidence that the apes in any of the experimental projects ever do any of this [proper ASL syntax] when signing. Stephen Anderson, *Doctor Dolittle's Delusion: Animals and the Uniqueness of Human Language* (Yale University Press: 2004) 297.

Then, Anderson goes on to expose the secrecy and lying from the researchers. He observes on Koko, "presented as the ape who 'really' learned sign language, and who uses it the way humans do—swearing, using metaphors, telling jokes, making puns." Well this is it! Apes can talk! Wait. He goes on, "But make no mistake, we have nothing but Patterson's word for any of this. She has not produced anything for anyone to look at except her summaries." These results are all "read in" by the

Earlier, Moses referred to "every tree that is pleasing to the sight." What does that mean? Not that it bore food—that's mentioned next—"or was good for food." So, to be pleasing to the eye means beauty—something you need a soul to understand. You can't write an algorithm for your computer to see or understand it. It's part of our creative aspect.

Creativity stands at the center of the arts. How many hours a day do you spend listening to music? According to Nielsen, Americans average four and a half hours a day.[2] And to this we should add the time spent on cinema and the fine arts.

For many, crafts and building things are outlets for creativity. Some people write imaginary stories, or nonfiction analytic works. Others explore history or philosophy. Scientists explore the natural world using their intellectual creativity and sophisticated instruments they also created.

Humans enjoy creativity. Successful creative work often results in intense pleasure. Creative people regularly strive for ever more impressive and beautiful works. New discoveries can lead to outright ecstasy.

Enjoying creativity isn't like sinful pleasures that degrade or harm people, like drugs, gluttony, or sexual immorality. Enjoying your creativity is gratifying but also nourishing. This is one of the great pleasures God wants us to enjoy.

Why aren't other animals this way? Bower birds build decorated nesting sites, but within clear limits. They are

---

researchers, who refuse to share their data or videos for scientific accountability. 285.

And, "The bottom line is that there is little or no evidence for any real combinatory structure in the productions of any of these animals." 297.

He correctly points to the real reason for overblown claims for talking animals: "Much research on animal communication has been driven by a need to show that there is nothing uniquely human about human natural language." 306.

[2] "We Listen to Music For More Than 4 1/2 Hours A Day, Nielsen Says" Marketingcharts.com, Nov. 13, 2017. They add, "Millennials are even more engaged: they use 3.8 devices during the typical week to listen, and average almost 40 hours per week.

immediately recognizable. A spider may spin a beautiful web, but we can identify species of spiders by their webs.

Even when we sit back and watch TV or browse, we are enjoying someone else's creativity. It's safe to say that doing and enjoying human creativity is quite close to the center of our lives.

God is creative

All we have to do is look around to see the creativity of God. He obviously delights in creating. Page through a picture book on the universe. Or leaf through any number of nature picture books. You can see God enjoying his own creative work in Genesis as he repeatedly stands back and says (probably with a smile) "It is good."

Look within yourself and see what David saw, "I am fearfully and wonderfully made; Wonderful are your works, And my soul knows it very well" (Psalm 139:14).

Creativity in heaven

God will never stop creating, and neither will we. The joy of creativity will be an important component in our everlasting ability to enjoy life in a growing way. God will probably dazzle us over and over again with spectacular creations. I'm thinking about taking up a musical instrument. Heck, maybe I'll take up several!

Regaining creativity

A growing Christian is a creative Christian. Under God we understand our creativity for what it's supposed to be—not an ego trip, not an ingenious pathway to more advanced weapons, or new ways to explain God away.

Under God, we finally understand the true beauty of all that we, as human image-bearers, are able to create. By studying God's creativity we can enhance our own.

As those to whom God gave the word of reconciliation (2 Corinthians 5:19), we should also be using our creativity to communicate the gospel. If all Christian songs sound alike, that's a huge problem. How creative have Christians been in reaching lost people?

One of the biggest choke points for godly creativity is the clergy-laity model of ministry. Under this model, it's the preachers and the church staff who create (along with a few volunteers they recruit). Everyone else consumes. Modern believers often have no expectation on themselves in this area. It's someone else's job. As a result, ninety percent of Christian brilliance and creativity goes into people's businesses or studios serving the world.

The big picture

Human intellectual and artistic creativity are so pronounced and amazing—so different than anything found in any other species—that it cries out the reality of humans' souls.

Spiritual creatures in the image of God are so amazing they can fly—all the way to the moon! They visit the bottom of the deepest ocean. But no sooner did they comprehend nuclear physics than they used it to destroy entire cities and threaten the planet.

Human creativity is fallen today, so it often produces ugly things. But even so, the paradox is clear. The most sublime literature, art, technology, and music come from the same creature. Because of our creativity, humans are far more destructive and violent than any other species by a very wide margin.

This paradox is the result of our high order creation. We not only have amazing powers to create beauty, but also a moral nature in revolt against God. Therefore, that brilliance has been turned to evil much of the time.

16 Humans Can Experience Union

Genesis 2:23-24

> And the man said, "This is now bone of my bones, and flesh of my flesh; she shall be called woman, because she was taken out of man." For this cause a man shall leave his father and his mother, and shall cleave to his wife; and the two shall become one flesh. (Genesis 2:23-24)

God created humans as sexual beings and he ordained the family, made up of one man and one woman and their offspring. The expression, "and the two shall become one flesh," describes a union relationship. Two individuals experiencing unity with one another is exclusively possible for spiritual beings.

You immediately see that sexuality is different for people than for others mammals. Here, the purpose of sex isn't procreation (contrary to some mistaken Christian teaching). For us, the purpose of sex to celebrate a union relationship.

God has unity and diversity

Up until now, every major feature in humans has corresponded to the same feature in God. But now that symmetry is broken.

God, as revealed in the Old Testament, is not sexual. Here is the only case in ancient religion of such a God. All the deities from surrounding nations had wife or husband gods. Sex and fertility were seen as central to religions based on nature.

With the Bible we have monotheism. Although they used the male pronoun, because they couldn't use the neuter (he's not an "it") he is essentially sexless.

Francis Schaeffer sees correspondence with this feature in the Trinity.[1] Because God is triune, he is one, yet he is three. He has unity and diversity at the same time. This answers an important question: How can God be personal, infinite, and self-existent at the same time? If he's personal, that implies relating to other persons. That would mean he *needs* his creation to avoid loneliness. That's not self-existent (which means he has no needs that he doesn't meet himself).

But as a triune God, this problem disappears in a puff of smoke. Only the Bible's unique picture of a triune God can fulfill this picture of a self-existent God who is also personal. Jesus referred to the love the Father had with him before the foundations of the world (John 17:24).

Although we read it in the previous chapter, the time setting for God's final statement in Chapter 1:31 is at the *end* of the sixth day. So it was at this point, after creating woman and presenting her to Adam that God said that everything he had created was "very good."

Union recovered

Becoming one with another personal being—it's one of the longings of our souls. We were made with this capability, and we will feel some loneliness if we lack it, even when we are surrounded by people.

God created humans with the ability to be individual selves, but also with the ability to fuse with another in a union relationship as this passage suggests. This ability and need are part of our architecture. It's why Adam being alone was "not good."

---

[1] Francis Schaeffer, *Genesis in Space and Time: The Flow of Biblical History,* (Wheaton: InterVarsity Press, 1972) 28.

Marriage is not the only way to experience a union relationship. Our need to experience union can be met in the first place in Christ. Paul says, "The one who joins himself to the Lord is one spirit with Him" (1 Corinthians 6:17). This union relationship with Jesus satisfies our inner desire to fuse with someone—to know and be known fully. This fusion with Jesus is the result of spiritual baptism, which puts us into Christ (1 Corinthians 12:13).

We also can enjoy substantial union with fellow believers in the body of Christ. In Romans 12:5 Paul says, "We, who are many, are one body in Christ, and individually members of one another." This "mystical union" with Jesus and one another in the body of Christ is deep and profound. We only gradually come to realize how deep it is in experience. Of course, if believers don't bother to build into community, they won't experience union at the level God intended.

Sexuality

But there's more for many of us. A marriage, and the family that results, should also become enjoyable, union relationships. Unfortunately, even evangelical Christians are turning away from this view.[2]

---

[2]Sociologist David Ayers demonstrates from the highly respected General Social Survey (GSS), in 2014 through 2018 that "only 37% of [self-identified] 'fundamentalist' adults said that "sex outside marriage was 'always wrong,' while 41% said it was 'not wrong at all.'" He also found that 86% of conservative protestant females and 82% of males had sex with one or more partners outside of marriage. David Ayers, "Current Sexual Practices of Evangelical Teens and Young Adults," *Institute for Family Research, Research Brief,* August 2019, 1.

Today, our culture has decided marriage isn't realistic, as witnessed by the wholesale decline of marriage in the West. Sociologists are tracking a decline of half a million marriages.[3] Even those who still dare to try marriage

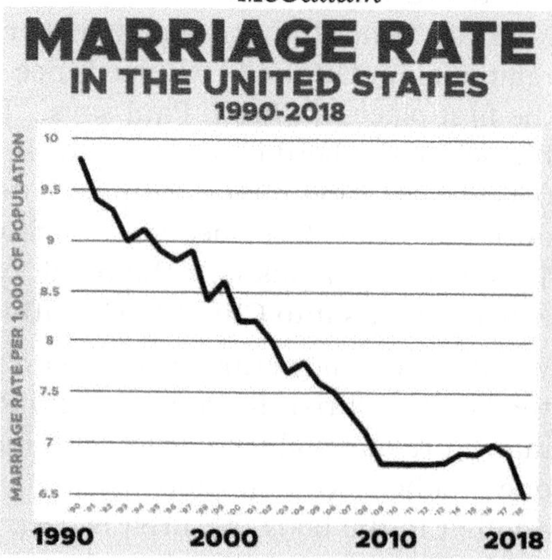

only do so after multiple other sex partners and a time living together. Wrong! And the research bears out the poverty of the modern way.[4]

God personally married the first couple here in Genesis 2. And according to Jesus, this set the pattern for marriage:

> Haven't you read that at the beginning the Creator 'made them male and female,' and said, 'For this reason a man will leave his father and mother and be united to his wife, and the two will become one

---

[3]Since reaching its peak in the early 1980s "the total number of people getting married has fallen steadily. Now only about two million marriages happen a year, a drop of almost half a million from their peak." Jay L. Zagorsky, "Why are fewer people getting married?" PBS.org. For chart, "USA - Marriage rate 1990-2018" Published by Erin Duffin, Jan 2, 2020, Statista.com. "In 2018, the marriage rate in the United States stood at 6.5 per 1,000 people of the population. This is a decrease from 1990 levels, when the marriage rate was 9.8 marriages per 1,000 people." That's a drop by one third.

[4]Rhoades and Stanley report, "Men and women who only slept with their (future) spouse prior to marriage reported higher marital quality than those who had other sexual partners as well." That makes sense, because it's the closest to a unity relationship. But most fornicators don't fit this picture: "In our sample, only 23 percent of the individuals who got married over the course of the study had had sex solely with the person they married." You also see what scripture would predict: "The more sexual partners a woman had had before marriage, the less happy she reported her marriage to be." Defying God's pattern only illustrates how right it is. Galena K. Rhoades and Scott M. Stanley "Before 'I Do' What Do Premarital Experiences Have to Do with Marital Quality Among Today's Young Adults?" *The National Marriage Project*, (University of Virginia, 2019) http://nationalmarriageproject.org.

> flesh'? So they are no longer two, but one. Therefore what God has joined together, let man not separate." (Matthew 19:4-6)

Notice a few things in this passage. First, Jesus says, "The Creator said...." So this wasn't Adam or Moses speaking, it was God himself who pronounced the two becoming one.

Secondly, Jesus was responding to a trap question about marriage and divorce. In reply, he acknowledges that Moses permitted divorce "because of the hardness of your hearts." But he quickly adds, "But it was not this way from the beginning" (v.8). In other words, this event in Genesis 2 defines marriage from God's point of view.

That pattern involves one man and one woman, not same sex, not groups. Both were virgins when entering marriage, not sleeping around for years before marriage. Both were ready to give themselves completely to the marriage.

The cost of departure

Marriage has suffered from humanity's fall away from God's will, and it's suffering more from the impact of modernity. It's harder to put a successful marriage together today. Our selfish sin natures cause us to approach marriage wrongly, seeking self-gratification. People come into marriage as love takers, not love givers. And in many cases, they come in with a history of damaging, sinful events in their pasts. Divorce, as Jesus said, is one such possibility. This a key reason why second marriages after divorce are far less successful than other marriages.[5]

---

[5]"In the last 50 years, the percentage of men and women who cohabit before marriage... has increased by almost 900 percent. Today 70 percent of women aged 30 to 34 have cohabited with a male partner, and two-thirds of new marriages take place between couples who have already lived together for an average of 31 months." Arielle Kuperberg, "Does Premarital Cohabitation Raise Your Risk of Divorce?" *Council on Contemporary Families*, March 10, 2014. Even defenders of divorce admit, "Statistics show that in the U.S., 50% percent of first marriages, 67% of second, and 74% of third marriages end in divorce." That's two thirds of second and three quarters of third marriages ending in divorce! (*Wevorce.com*, 09 Jan 2017).

But even more common in our culture are people approaching marriage with a past history of multiple previous sex partners. This is a violation of God's pattern for marriage, even when the previous partner is your spouse.

The idea of trial marriages, living together, as a way to predict later success in marriage is hugely mistaken. And the results prove it. Marriages after cohabiting are markedly lower in survival than marriages without cohabitation.[6]

In addition to these strikes against marriage, we see increasingly common abusive sexual encounters inflicted on the young. These violent events can harm people's ability to love and trust at a deep level.

The modern world has completely forsaken God's pattern for marriage, but that's no excuse for those of us who follow God. We have his word and the power of the Holy Spirit. Through authentic spiritual growth, God can heal even the worst damage done in a fallen world.

By God's grace we can see successful marriages become the norm in the body of Christ. In the relatively few cases of demise, the seeds of failure were plain enough long before the marriage finally failed—usually, departure from God's pattern here in Genesis 2. The body of Christ needs to come together to support and nurture marriage and families as the critical indispensable pathway to healthy lives for our members.

Paul also goes to this passage as the key to understanding marriage:

> So husbands ought also to love their own wives as their own bodies. He who loves his own wife loves himself; for no one ever hated his own flesh, but

---

[6]This remains true today, notwithstanding claims by some studies that cohabitation either no longer correlates with divorce, or that only measuring or selection bias explained the correlation earlier. See Michael J. Rosenfeld and Katharina Roesler "Cohabitation Experience and Cohabitation's Association With Marital Dissolution," *Journal of Marriage and Family*, 24 September 2018, 1.

> nourishes and cherishes it, just as Christ also does
> the church, because we are members of His body.
> (Ephesians 5:28-30)

Wait. Is he talking about marriage or the body of Christ? You can see the concepts are intertwined here. The union relationship between Jesus and his body is analogous to the union between man and wife. And how does he know that?

> For this reason a man shall leave his father and
> mother and shall be joined to his wife, and the two
> shall become one flesh. This mystery is great; but I
> am speaking with reference to Christ and the
> church. (Ephesians 5:31-32)

You can see where he gets it—right here in Genesis 2.

Union and self-giving love

Sex is supposed to be a celebration of this union relationship. That's why the picture is shattered by promiscuity. Promiscuity signals selfishness. When people sleep around it's because they want self-gratification, but they don't want commitment. They don't understand or want union, or they mistakenly believe that sleeping around won't harm their ability to be united later.

But selfish pleasure is no substitute for union. Promiscuous sex leaves people unsatisfied, but more desirous than ever. At the same time, walls of self-protection rise up as promiscuous people reel backward from the pain they experience.

Sexual immorality also compromises your future ability to give yourself fully in a marriage. You're setting a pattern of sex as a chance to take love—the pornographic ideal. But married love is nothing like that. The library of erotic images in your mind will continue to interfere with your sex life in marriage. God never intended you to compare your spouse with other sex partners.

Today the pornographic ideal competes with godly sex. Successful, godly sex involves a mature, committed human love relationship, and we don't learn that while sleeping around or gaping at pornography.

It's a good thing that Jesus changes lives. Substantial healing is possible if you submit yourself to the great physician. Even years of damage can be undone, at least enough for you to succeed in marriage.

Afterlife

In the eternal state, union relationships are not ended, they're enhanced. Jesus is going to be right there where we can enjoy him at a new level. Eternal union with other believers is also part of the picture. The friendships we develop with fellow believers today are eternal friendships. Loneliness will be at an end.

The big picture

Experiencing union with God and his people feels good. It opens doors to deeper sharing and trust. Relationships can deepen. Every day we can come before God and have him open our eyes and hearts to sense his oneness with us at deeper levels. As we mature, we also have the best chance of succeeding in marriage.

17 Humans: Shameless and Uninhibited

Genesis 2:25

> And the man and his wife were both naked and were not ashamed. (Genesis 2:25)

Why point out their nakedness? It becomes clear when you see them after the fall (in Chapter 3) trying to sew fig leaves into loincloths. Can you imagine how pathetic that must have looked? They knew nothing of sewing. And fig leaves are not the large banana fronds pictured in Sunday school brochures. A fig leaf is far smaller. What a picture of our pathetic efforts to hide our guilt.

Why do people feel guilty? Is it the wrongful demands of their family of origin? Is it social pressure and putdowns? Not if we can believe Genesis. None of those things were present in this story. According to this account, they felt guilty because they *were* guilty, just like we are.

God created people who were at peace with themselves, happy with themselves, and with each other. They saw no reason why anything needed to change.

They were also at one with God. You see no sign of any tension or any problems until Chapter 3. When sin came in they felt the need to cover up and hide from God.

God is unashamed

It's probably unnecessary to point out that God doesn't suffer from shame. He is happy with who he is and what he does. He's confident that he's in the right

God knows that shamelessness is important for good relationships. Shame immediately shuts down open relating, and that's a key reason why Satan fosters as much guilt and shame as possible. He is known as "the accuser of the brethren" (Revelation 12:10).

The entrance of guilt and shame draws one's attention to self. The awareness that something is wrong with me makes me self-conscious and anxious. The result is inhibition. We can't act normally. We're self-protective. The author here clearly emphasizes the importance of shamelessness.

Shamelessness recovered

Incredibly, in Christ we can find release from shame. If we believe what God says about our position in Jesus, we realize we are "the righteousness of God in him"
(2 Corinthians 5:21).

Paul teaches that the key to walking in "a newness of life" is believing who we are in Christ—that "we have been buried with him through baptism into death, so that as Christ was raised from the dead through the glory of the Father, so we too might walk in newness of life" (Romans 6:4).

It's not easy, because our position in Christ is so counter-intuitive. But the teaching is unmistakable in one passage after another. Jesus paid a tremendous price to win our innocence before God, and the free access that comes with it.

As believers grow, they learn how to approach God only in Christ, never through their works. Free grace applies to spiritual growth, not just to initial forgiveness. It takes real faith to believe what God says about you, rather than believing your feelings about yourself. But as you learn to come in helplessness regarding your flesh, you will gradually learn how to draw your strength from him.

Heaven

When God says, "Behold, I am making all things new," (Revelation 21:5) it includes our fallen nature. People in heaven finally and fully regain freedom from guilt and shame. No longer will our sin nature fill our minds with lust and regret. God himself is right there, and we will feel no need to cower before him.

We won't feel any need to shift blame by accusing others. We'll have no reason or desire to lie. Imagine how awesome it will be to relate to our friends and to God in completely shameless freedom!

The big picture

Adam and Eve were free to frolic through the woods and the garden in complete freedom—never a thought about self-doubt, never a need to introspect, never lacking confidence, and able to give full attention to each other.

Already today, believers can begin to feel that freedom in a measure, and we should feel excited when we anticipate the complete freedom to come.

18 The Two Trees

Genesis 2:16-17

> Out of the ground the Lord God caused to grow every tree that is pleasing to the sight and good for food; the tree of life also in the midst of the garden, and the tree of the knowledge of good and evil. (Genesis 2:9)

We now come to the two trees God created and consider their unusual names.

The forbidden tree

Think about the name God gave the forbidden tree: "the tree of the knowledge of good and evil." That's a long name; a careful name. What is God signaling here? What's wrong with knowing good and evil?

First, it's not the tree of knowledge, as some commentators have mistakenly said. This is a special kind of knowledge. Knowing good and evil is clearly an aspect of humans with souls and free moral agency. But didn't they have that before the fall? Is this suggesting they were non-moral beings before the fall? No.

Others have mistakenly suggested that this was the experiential knowledge of evil—that they now knew evil, not as a theory, but as their own experience. But Chapter 3:22 says, "Then the Lord God said, 'Behold, the man has become like one of Us, knowing good and evil.'" The "Us" again refers to the triune God. It's not the angels. But the important point for our question is the phrase "like one of us, knowing good and evil." God doesn't know evil experientially. He has never done anything evil.

So what is this knowledge of good and evil that's so bad? The key is what God says, "They (the humans) have become like one of us." How does God know evil or good? He simply looks within. He doesn't look to any external standard to know these things. There is no such standard. The standard is God himself.

Now, humans "have become like one of us." Earlier, Adam received his knowledge of good and evil from God when he said, "From any tree of the garden you may eat freely; but from the tree of the knowledge of good and evil you shall not eat... (Genesis 2:16-17).

Adam needed no research project to discover right and wrong. No reading. No introspection. All he needed to do was ask God. God was his source of moral knowledge.

Now, when they partook of this tree, they have "become like one of us," i.e. they simply looked within to discover good and evil. They didn't need to ask God. They were now creating their own moral norms based on self.

Already they had decided that being naked was wrong. That's what God called attention to: "Who told you that you were naked? Have you eaten from the tree of which I commanded you not to eat?" (Genesis 3:11).[1] The fact that they were creating their own arbitrary moral norms clearly signaled that they had partaken of the forbidden fruit. None of the other animals wore clothes. This idea came from within.

Ever since that day, morality and religion became something humans can create without reference to the true God. In our day, the consensus is that faith is a choice people make, completely independent of whether any of it is true. No one, including God, should question the validity of another's faith choice or their moral values.

---

[1]Several times in Chapter 3 God asks questions. Openness theologians take this to mean that he didn't know where Adam and Eve were hiding or whether they had eaten of the forbidden tree! This view is ludicrous. He only asks them questions so they have the opportunity to come forward and confess.

This is called autonomy. Autonomy means literally "self-law" or "self-rule" (from *autos* = self; *nomos* = law). When people become a law unto themselves, they generate morals and truth from within. At that point, literally *anything* can happen. Even Hitler had a moral system—a twisted one, that he created himself. But he strongly argued for doing right and not doing wrong according to that self-generated moral system, clearly spelled out in *Mein Kampf.*

This autonomy was at the center of what Satan offered them earlier: "God knows that in the day you eat from it your eyes will be opened, and you will be like God, knowing good and evil." So Satan, who prizes autonomy so much he turned against God himself, also pedals it to humans today, just like he did then. There remains one barrier to autonomy—God. That's why so many hate him.

The good tree

Next we have the tree of life. This tree stands for eternal life, according to Chapter 3:22: "Now, he might stretch out his hand, and take also from the tree of life, and eat, and live forever." It's not a magic, life-giving tree, because God is the giver of life; not trees. So the tree meant choosing life with God or death apart from God. He could have laid two candy bars out there with the same instructions and the same effect.

Adam and Eve were sinless before their fall, so they could have enjoyed eternal life even without the cross. All they had to do was follow God. Their freedom was complete—they could do whatever they wanted with only one, single exception—partaking of the forbidden fruit.

The opposite of life is death. To the Hebrews, death didn't mean annihilation, but separation. Separation of the soul from the body is physical death. Separation from God is spiritual death—the consequence of the fall.

God's ideal for humans was life, as is clear throughout the Bible. Of Jesus, it is said, "In him was life and the life was the light of men" (John 1:4). The ones who believe in Jesus, "will not perish, but have eternal life" (John 3:16).

In heaven

We finally find the tree of life reappearing in heaven, where eternal life is finally realized. Jesus said to John, "He who has an ear, let him hear what the Spirit says to the churches. To him who overcomes, I will grant to eat of the tree of life which is in the Paradise of God" (Revelation 2:7).

Sure enough, when John sees the New Heaven and Earth, there's the tree of life: "Then he showed me a river of the water of life, clear as crystal, coming from the throne of God and of the Lamb, in the middle of its street. On either side of the river was the tree of life, bearing twelve kinds of fruit, yielding its fruit every month; and the leaves of the tree were for the healing of the nations" (Revelation 22:1-2).

Is it a literal tree that people go out and eat from? That's doubtful. The book of Revelation is apocalyptic literature, where symbols abound. He often has to have an angel next to him to explain the symbols. It's a real vision depicting real future history, not fiction. But it teaches about the future through symbols, most of which come from the Old Testament, like this one.

Two dichotomies

The two trees imply two dichotomies: good and evil and life and death. These are connected in that evil led to death. But the same cannot be said for human good. Only the good deeds Jesus did overcame human evil and death.

Paul says, "For since by a man came death, by a man also came the resurrection of the dead. For as in Adam all die, so also in Christ all will be made alive" (1 Corinthians 15:21-22). He goes on to say that death is Jesus' final foe—not yet completely conquered (1 Corinthians 15:26).

Once humans abandoned God's way, only the seed of woman (Jesus) could "wash their robes [forgiveness], so that they may have the right to the tree of life" (Revelation 22:14).

The big picture

By the end of Chapter 2 God has reached the conclusion of his work of creation. He has created the marvelous human creatures, living in their own lush garden, with all the advantages we've covered.

It seems unlikely that anything will go wrong. After all, they have each other. They have abundant sources of food. God is their friend and provider. Only one tree was forbidden. Why would they go to that tree?

19 The Lead-up to the Fall

Genesis 3:1-5

A world with no fall

Many are unaware that the biblical teaching, that humanity fell away from God, is unique and missing from most religions. That's a major problem. The fall of humanity from God's will is a crucial element in the biblical worldview, answering so many important questions.

Because of the fall, humans come with an inborn fallen nature. It's a sin nature that inclines us to reject God's leadership, to be selfish, to be dishonest, and hostile. Consider the difference, depending on whether your worldview includes a fall.

Without the fall:

With no fall, the world is normal, and as it should be. For theistic religions that advance a creator God, the evil we see on earth would be part of God's design. This really means that such a creator God is ultimately the author of human evil.

With the fall:

Under the biblical view that a real fall happened, the world is abnormal, and broken. Under this view, God is not the author of evil. Rather, he was the author of human freedom. Humans authored evil (after Satan had earlier).

We saw earlier that God knew the fall was coming, and he created anyway. So God considered authentic freedom so valuable that it was worth the price. No doubt, part of God's decision was that he knew he had a plan to rescue to people in the grip of evil.

The serpent

We read that "the serpent was the shrewdest of all the creatures the Lord God had made" (Genesis 3:1). Is this non-historical mythopoeic writing like Jack and the bean stock?[1] Before jumping to that conclusion, notice the following:

- Revelation 12:10 talks about "the dragon," explaining that he is "the serpent of old who is called the devil and Satan." So the serpent is Satan, or is indwelt by Satan.

- We know animals can be demon possessed, according to Mark 5:13, where Jesus sent demons into some pigs.

- We know animals can speak when a spiritual being speaks through them, because in Numbers 22:28 God spoke through a donkey.

- All the other figures in this account in Genesis 3 seem normal and historical. The snake is the only odd part.

- We know that angels often appear as humans and therefore could probably appear as a different animal.

We conclude that this account is historical, not mythical. Maybe Satan appeared as a serpent, or spoke through a serpent. But the point is, this story actually happened. It's pointless to try to read the Bible without facing the reality of the supernatural, and that's really the only problem with this account.

Satan is a real being, a cherub—one of the greatest angelic beings (Ezekiel 28:14). Without a real Satan, the whole

---

[1] The "mythopoeic" genre refers to the typical mode of storytelling seen in ancient religions where anything goes. For instance in the Iliad, a river leaps from its boundaries and chases Achilles. In the Babylonian creation myth, the Enuma Elish, the god, Marduk slays a female deity named Tiamat and divides her body thus creating land and sea. Alexander Heidel, *The Babylonian Genesis: The Story of Creation,* Second Edition (Chicago: University of Chicago Press, 1963) 17ff.

storyline of scripture is shredded. Yet as many as sixty percent of self-described "born again Christians" don't believe he exists![2]

You can see he is already fallen when he shows up in this story, so fallenness didn't begin with humans. We saw earlier that, according to Ezekiel 28:13, Satan had some connection with "Eden, the garden of God" before he was fallen. Under the gap theory of creation, Eden could have been a recreation of an earlier garden. Or, did Satan's fall happen more recently, after God created Eden here in Genesis? We don't know, and it's not important.

The attack

The serpent speaks: "Really?" he asked the woman. "Did God really say you must not eat any of the fruit in the garden?" (Genesis 3:1). It's not hard to see that he's already planting a suggestion. How strange God is! Why would he be so restrictive? What's wrong with him? But he knows exactly what God said. He's spinning what was said, hoping Eve would be careless and not notice.

His approach is different than one might expect. You could imagine him saying, "Nice fruit! That's probably got awesome flavor." No, that's for later. His first focus is on the question, "What has God said?"

The word of God is so central in our relationship with him. Can we trust his word? When we speak of biblical faith, we aren't talking about an arbitrary belief based on our wishful thinking. Biblical faith is believing God's word—that it's true, and that I can rely on it. Satan knows that. And he knows that if Eve gives any ground on this point, she won't be able to resist more slippage.

---

[2] Phil Zuckerman, "The Secular Life: The Devil? Seriously? How can people believe the manifestly absurd?" *Psychology Today*, Sep. 28, 2015.

Eve's reply

Eve replies, "Of course we may eat fruit from the trees in the garden. It's only the fruit from the tree in the middle of the garden that we are not allowed to eat. God said, 'You must not eat it or even touch it; if you do, you will die'" (v. 2-3).

Curiously, she has information we didn't get in the earlier account of God's warning (see 1:17). He never said anything about not touching the forbidden fruit. But God spoke that to Adam. Eve wasn't around yet. Did Eve get her information from Adam? Probably. And is this discrepancy—between what God said in the text and what she said—significant?

I think it might be. At least we know from church and Jewish history that when people add to God's word, what they add tends to be more restrictive than the original. Christian leaders will note that alcoholism ruins lives and families, and conclude, "Since this is dangerous, we'd probably be better off if we just don't allow drinking at all." And later, "In fact we probably shouldn't even enter a place that serves alcohol. Then we'll be real safe."

The problem with this train of thought is that people are increasingly confronted with what Francis Schaeffer called "arbitrary absolutes." These become barriers to faith, as non-believing people see following God as very restrictive—way more than it really is. Here, Satan is already trying to convince Eve that God is unnecessarily restrictive, and for self-serving reasons.

When Jesus was attacked by Satan in the wilderness, Jesus countered his attack repeatedly saying, "it is written," we don't see any such discrepancy with God's word. Proverbs 30:5-6 says,

> Every word of God proves true. He is a shield to all who come to him for protection. Do not add to his words, or he may rebuke you and expose you as a liar.

Most of the objectionable parts of medieval Christianity, for instance, are additions to scripture. And many current church practices are also off-putting to non-believers, and those are also usually not based on scripture. Adding to scripture is a bad idea. Paul says in 1 Corinthians 4 that the purpose of his argument is so that "you may learn not to exceed what is written" (v. 6)

The words of God are very important, and powerful. If we are careless with his words, it can cause power to shift. Satan must comply with God's word when it properly applies. That's why he had to give up tempting Jesus (Luke 4:13).

Satan denies the word of God

> And the serpent said to the woman, "You surely shall not die! For God knows that in the day you eat from it your eyes will be opened, and you will be like God, knowing good and evil." (Genesis 3:4-5)

After questioning God's word, the Evil One now denies it outright. So his first claim is that God is a liar. And to bolster that claim, he offers his alternative explanation: "God knows that in the day you eat from it your eyes will be opened, and you will be like God, knowing good and evil" (v. 5).

So according to the Evil One, God's lie—that the fruit was fatal—was actually to cover up the truth—that the fruit makes you like God.

When analyzing this claim, we first notice it's partially true. God confirms that it's true in Genesis 3:22 when he said, "Behold, the man has become like one of us, knowing good and evil...." But Satan's lie was his implication that trying to become like God is a good thing. He implied that God is jealous and self-serving; that he doesn't want others to have the prerogatives he has.

So whether it's God lying, or that he is selfishly clinging to his prerogatives, Satan is accusing God. That's what he does. His title "the devil" comes from a word (*diabolos*) that means a slanderer or accuser.

Satan is aggressive. He's leading a revolt against God and that requires that people be suspicious of God. When you analyze Satan's approach in this story, you see that his claims have nothing to do with the forbidden fruit. They have everything to do with God. Whatever God is, he clearly can't be trusted. Suspicion, or distrust, breaks down relationships. The Evil One knows that he has to sow suspicion if people are to turn away from their own creator.

The dynamics of the lie

Part of the genius of his lying in this story comes from including truthful content, but leaving out key points that change the picture dramatically.

For instance in this story, he left out key facts:

- That they were finite and therefore unqualified to be their own god.

- That they lacked the fixed attribute of goodness like God has. They were changeable, and therefore anything, including the worst atrocities, could happen if they went this way.

- That by throwing off God's authority, they would also be throwing off his protection.

- That going this way would not teach them what good and evil are, but would leave them in moral confusion.

- That although they would be superficially similar to God in one way, they could never be like God in most ways.

- That they may no longer be followers of God, but instead, they would become slaves to the most ruthless master, Satan himself!

So, although God later agreed that they now were like him in that they could "know" good and evil from within, instead of from referring to God, the larger picture is false. They were really nothing like God.

The big picture

This passage is important for several reasons. One is for our understanding of Satan. In the millennia since this episode, nothing has changed in Satan's approach. We saw earlier that he seeks to undercut trust with his accusations and lies. Trust can also be translated as faith. The one thing God calls on us for—saving faith, or trust—is the thing the Evil One goes after. Why would you follow a leader you don't trust? You might comply outwardly in order to avoid trouble. But you would not cleave to God in love if you distrust him.

20 The Fall

Genesis 3:6-7

The humans cross over

> When the woman saw that the fruit of the tree was good for food and pleasing to the eye, and also desirable for gaining wisdom, she took some and ate it. She also gave some to her husband, who was with her, and he ate it. (v. 6)

You can see from this verse that something horrible has already happened in Eve's heart—she has believed Satan. You can see this from the fact that she looked at the fruit and thinks, "it was desirable for gaining wisdom" (v 6).

Where did that come from? God never told her the fruit would make her wise. He said it would make you dead. This has to be a reference to Satan's proposition that they could know good and evil. She has equated knowing good and evil with gaining wisdom.

Once a person begins to disbelieve God, whether a lot or a little, all resistance to evil collapses. Her other observations—that the fruit was "good for food and pleasing to the eye" wouldn't have carried much weight unless she was doubting God in her heart.

And she was doubting him a lot. It's clear she believed God was a liar, because she didn't think the fruit would kill her. And if she believed that, she must have also accepted Satan's reason for why God lied—that he was holding out on humans and keeping them down. Otherwise, she would have had no reason to think it would make them wise. If it was true that God was holding out and repressing humans, he clearly couldn't be trusted.

So unbelief—distrust of God—bursts onto the scene, and they now have no resistance to temptation.

The fall and the kosmos

Eve looked up at the forbidden fruit and she saw three attractive things. They happen to match three values that characterize the world system according to the apostle John:

> Do not love the world nor the things in the world. If anyone loves the world, the love of the Father is not in him. For all that is in the world, the lust of the flesh and the lust of the eyes and the boastful pride of life, is not from the Father, but is from the world. The world is passing away, and also its lusts; but the one who does the will of God lives forever. (1 John 2:15-17)

Jesus called Satan "ruler of this world" (John 12:31). The world, or *kosmos* is Satan's kingdom according to the New Testament. He captivates people's hearts by appealing to them with the values mentioned here in 1 John.

When Eve looked up to the forbidden fruit, "she saw that it was good for food." That's eerily similar to "the lust of the flesh." She also saw it was "a delight to the eyes" which sounds similar to "the lust of the eye." And she saw that it was "desirable to make one wise" which, in context, refers to Satan's promise that she could be like God. So, this matches "the boastful pride of life."

It's doubtful that this is pure coincidence. Neither is it a coincidence when Satan attacked Jesus in the wilderness (Luke 4:1-13). He tempted Jesus to turn stones into bread (the lust of the flesh, especially after forty days fasting). He showed him the glory and splendor of the world all its kingdoms (the lust of the eye). And he dared him to show off at the temple (the boastful pride of life).

It's not that Moses, Luke, and John lined these accounts up. Rather, the reason is that Satan works in predictable ways, and he knows how humans work. But none of these values would have gained traction with Eve unless she had already begun to distrust God.

Who was with her?

So Eve "took from its fruit and ate; and she gave also to her husband with her, and he ate" (v. 6). Wait, he was with her? Are we seriously to believe that Adam was standing right there the whole time? If so, this is a staggering failure. It would mean Adam was so passive that he might as well have been a drooling zombie!

Yet, when the serpent says "you" throughout the dialog, he uses the plural. That would normally mean both of them were standing there. How could Adam listen to this creature urging his wife to violate God's will and say nothing? And then, passively take one of the fruits from her hand and eat it. At least she put up some kind of fight. But with no support of any kind from her weakling husband, she was in a bad situation.

It's possible that he wasn't there. The Serpent could have used the plural in his absence, as though he's talking to her about "ya'll." The last phrase "who was with her" could mean she gave it to him when they got together, or he was with her in a more general sense, being in the garden.

Whether he was with her or not, the New Testament consistently blames Adam for the fall. This is in contrast to early church fathers, who excoriated women for being the cause of the fall.[1] But that's wrong. It was "through one man" that the fall occurred (Romans 5:12). He was the one God instructed not to eat of the tree.

---

[1] Tertullian is typical, "Do you not know that each of you [women] is also an Eve? ...You are the devil's gateway, you are the unsealer of that forbidden tree, you are the first deserter of the divine law, you are the one who persuaded him who the devil was too weak to attack. How easily you destroyed man, the image of God. Because of the death which you brought upon us, even the Son of God had to die." Gaius Tertullian, "On the Apparel of Women" Book 1, ch.1, 1.

> She took from its fruit and ate; and she gave also to
> her husband with her, and he ate. At that moment,
> their eyes were opened, and they suddenly felt
> shame at their nakedness. So they strung fig leaves
> together around their hips to cover themselves.
> (Genesis 3:6-7)

At the moment the first humans ate the forbidden fruit
their union with God was ruptured. The devastating effects
were instantly evident, and I like Schaeffer's analysis: that
the key aftermath is alienation.[2]

Psychological alienation

The text says their eyes were opened, but to what? Instead
of some glorious vision, they cringe back in shame at what
they see. Their eyes were instantly opened to their own sin
and the shame that came with it. They felt a horrifying
discomfort with what they were. You see an immediate urge
to cover up. Guilt and the shame that goes with it must
have been a sickening shock for these people who had
never known shame.

Here is a crucial result of the fall: it puts self at the center.
Everything is about self. Even others are there to serve the
interests of self. But God didn't design us to have self at the
center. That place is reserved for God, and when self
replaces God, an awful distortion results.

So now we have self-absorbed people, and they aren't
happy with what they see inside. Like people ever since,
self-absorption leads to dissatisfaction. They immediately
create the notion of doing away with nakedness. Humans
are alone among higher animals to this day in feeling too
awkward and embarrassed to walk around naked. Even
oral tribes that are mostly naked cover their genitals.

Their fig leaf coverings must have looked ridiculous. They
knew nothing about sewing nor had any tools or materials.

---

[2]I am indebted here for the notion of several alienations to Francis Schaeffer,
Genesis in Space and Time, (InterVarsity Press, 1972).

Fig leaves have become well known in idiom, meaning a lame or weak excuse for wrongdoing.

Think about the absurdity of this event. Here is Adam, talking about their problem: "Okay, we've messed up here real bad, we've got a major problem coming up when God shows up... Let's cover our genitals!" As funny as that sounds, it matches a related fallen human practice—the formation of religion. Human-made religions help keep the focus away from the real issues and onto silly taboos and pointless rituals.

Fallen people don't know why they are the way they are. They feel their views are right, whether they really are right or not. They're not able to be objective, and they lack a fixed standard by which to understand the particulars around them. Internal deception is possible and highly likely. When reasoning out from self, all we can do is relativize every particular to self, or to other particulars. Knowing truth becomes an imaginary goal. I can only know what is true to me.

Psychological alienation; people ill at ease with themselves; fallen people feel a low grade negative sense that there must be more, that something is wrong. Often depressed, often anxious, often confused, always dissatisfied, never sure, people with fallen natures are psychologically sick. Some are worse than others. In addition to our natures, circumstances can add abuse, trauma, and abandonment to make matters worse.

Recovery

Again, as with other lost attributes, the psychological consequences of the fall can be substantially healed. The first step is to restore the ruptured connection with God. But even after coming to Jesus, this healing won't necessarily happen. Believers have to accept the need to grow in Christ and to commit to a healthy spiritual community.

The big picture

To heal the psychological alienation from the fall, self must be removed from the center. Jesus called this "dying to self" (John 12:25) or "losing yourself" (Luke 17:13). Understanding the negatives produced in the fall helps us see more clearly why things have to change.

Knowing and believing in our new identity in Jesus provides the base for the Holy Spirit to begin healing our self-absorption and begins teaching us God's answer to our psychological alienation—self-giving love. To move down this road, people need to build their grace-based relationship with God, but also deeper relationships in a community of God's people.

21 More Aftermath of the Fall

Genesis 3:8-24

Theological alienation

> Then the man and his wife heard the sound of the
> Lord God as he was walking in the garden in the cool
> of the day, and they hid from the Lord God among
> the trees of the garden. But the Lord God called to
> the man, "Where are you?" He answered, "I heard
> you in the garden, and I was afraid because I was
> naked; so I hid." (Genesis 3:8-10)

Here is the main source of destruction since the fall. The
good relationship we saw in Chapter 2 between humans
and God has been shattered. People are now separate from
God—a state amounting to spiritual death.[1] Again, shame
and the awareness of guilt sends fallen people fleeing from
the presence of a righteous God. When God comes walking,
they instantly realize accountability is at hand.

Every one of us can imagine ourselves doing the same thing
if we were in their shoes. They probably didn't know God
very well. What is he going to do? He already mentioned
death as the penalty for what they had done, so they were
probably expecting God would strike them dead. Actually,
as we read on, he is firm but surprisingly mild.

God called to Adam to come out, and when explaining why
they hid, Adam gave the excuse, "I was afraid because I was
naked; so I hid" (v. 10). God knew exactly what the
arbitrary moral standard implied.

---

[1] Young earth readers think God's warning that "in the day you eat of it you will
surely die," means there was no death before the fall. This is a misreading. God is
referring to the humans dying, not to all animals. Also, their death was spiritual
death, as seen from the fact that it happened, "in the day you eat of it." Physical
death also resulted later.

> And God said, "Who told you that you were naked?
> Have you eaten from the tree of which I commanded
> you not to eat?" (v. 11)

What an odd reason Adam gave for hiding—like God hadn't seen him naked already? His warped moral values clearly signaled that finite beings with no actual moral compass were generating the new norms.

God asked the pertinent question, "Who told you that you were naked?" It's so clear that they created this standard out of their own minds, and out of their damaged and bruised souls, reeling from personal sin and shame.

Dishonesty

Equally evident is Adam's new trait of dishonesty. "Yeah God, our willful disobedience of your clear instructions had nothing to do with our hiding from you. It was just because we were naked!"

Being naked is not the reason they hid. Nakedness is something that happened to them—they had no responsibility for it. So, by diverting the explanation away from his own sinful moral choices to something he never chose, Adam lies to God. This form of lying is blame-shifting (away from himself and onto God, who made him naked) and rationalization (because his actions are not the result of personal wrongdoing).

God asks the obvious follow up question. "Have you eaten from the tree?" Again, he put it in a question, although it's painfully clear he knows the answer (contrary to open theism). He asks because he's giving Adam and Eve a chance to confess.

Surely Adam will fall on his knees and burst into tears, "Yes! You've got me! I did it Lord! Can you forgive me?"
No.

His reply exemplifies his new fallen nature: "The woman whom you gave to be with me, she gave me from the tree, and I ate" (v. 12). Adam is falling all over himself shifting the blame away from himself and onto Eve and even onto God himself. "Everything was fine until you gave me Eve."

Sociological alienation

"The woman whom you gave to be with me..." (v. 12). How quickly Adam throws Eve under the bus! It's her fault! Already, humans are demonstrating one of their most awful fallen traits—interpersonal and inter-factional hostility, finger pointing, and fighting.

This kind of alienation includes the inability to build successful love relationships. When two people come together, each with self at the center, they come to take, not to give. They may be willing to give a bit, as long as they get back even more. But this is not a formula for successful relationships.

All human history is also the history of murder, conquest, thievery, and war. No species on earth comes anywhere close to humans when it comes to slaying members of their own species.

We don't like to see ourselves this way. In 1986 people launched an event called "Hands Across America." They got millions of Americans to hold hands stretching from east to west coast across America as a celebration of human unity and fund raiser to fight poverty in Africa.

Although they failed to fill in all the gaps in the chain, close to six million people stood for fifteen minutes and sang a song, "We are the world," while swaying back and forth. Of the $34 million raised, only $15 million went to the poor, according The New York Times—so less than three dollars a head.

I thought the event was bizarre and even comical. But at the same time, I felt angry. Puzzled, I wondered why the event made me feel so angry. There was the obvious fact that they could have given far more to poverty in Africa without any need to stretch out and sing this way.

But upon more reflection, I realized that it offended me because it was so false. This strange picture of humanity—holding hands, smiling, and singing together about how awesome and unified they are—that's how humans would like to imagine themselves. But that picture flies directly in the face of history or any evening news report.

Ecological alienation

God addressed Adam:

> Cursed is the ground because of you; through painful toil you will eat of it all the days of your life. Both thorns and thistles it shall grow for you; and you will eat the plants of the field; by the sweat of your face you will eat bread, till you return to the ground, because from it you were taken; for you are dust, and to dust you shall return." (vs. 17-19)

Like God's other pronouncements, this one isn't announcing his desire, but the unfortunate consequences of sin. God often attributes negative events to his judgment, not because he caused them, but because he could have prevented them, and didn't.

When humans threw off the leadership of God, they also threw off his protection. That explains why humans suffer under killer storms, earthquakes, volcanoes, floods, droughts, and pandemics. Although wanting to be "like God" humans are just finite creatures with no power to control nature.

This is when humans became adversaries toward nature; not when they were created. Now, we see humans greedily stripping the land anywhere they go, eager to exploit. At other times we see humans huddling in fear before the overwhelming power of natural disaster, utterly unable to protect themselves.

God never gave the earth into human ownership. We don't own the planet, we are temporarily entrusted with it. The earth is a stewardship for human caretakers. Of course this view changed after the fall. People now believe they own their piece of earth absolutely, and can do whatever they want with it.

Other inner changes from the fall:

Satan told Eve she could "become like God." This was never possible except in the narrow sense of being autonomous. Now, instead of having God at the center, we see humans moving self to the center.

God is truly the center of the universe because he created it and sustains it. As such, he created humans to live in dependence on him. When humans put self in the place where God should be, it terribly distorted every trait God had earlier built in. Here is a breakdown of each earlier trait marking humans as being created in God's image. Notice how they changed when self went to the center.

God gave us a nature to enjoy	Becoming "like God" put self at the center
Benevolent leadership	When self went to the center, leading the world for its own good and under God's direction changed to dominating nature for selfish benefit. The focus went to how we can use nature for food, riches, weapons, or dwellings. You can see this particularly disturbing twist when humans destroy nature for fun— shooting animals because they are moving targets. Think of the American Bison. Within a few decades of exposure to the white man, this sixty million member species was on the brink of extinction. Accounts abound of trains stopping near a herd, and the passengers coming out to blast away, leaving the prairie covered with

	dead bison. They usually didn't even skin or butcher the dead animals. They just drove on, entertainment complete. What seems so pointless and crazy becomes even darker if it's true what many historians believe—that white people wanted to kill the bison in order to cut off the food source for the plains Indians. Humans are cruel, aggressive, and deadly.
	Other forms of destruction come from carelessness, where people spray poisons or slash and burn forests unlike any other creature.
	One of the most pronounced outcomes of the self-centered shift has been human thirst for power and control over other humans. Human history is a history of war, slaughter, enslavement, and atrocity. Most of these episodes are the result of human leadership distorted by the fall.
Accomplishment	God made humans with the desire to work toward useful goals. Accomplishing valid goals should bring pleasure. But since the fall, work has changed. Instead of being enjoyable, work in a fallen world became drudgery and pain. This is the significance of the "thorns and thistles."
	With the negative conditions in a fallen world, it takes all the work some can do just to survive on the extreme edge of starvation.
	For others, their work lives have become a way to establish their identity. They prove they're important because of how much "success" they've enjoyed.
	This leads to a striking fallen human

	characteristic—greed. Simply working because it's good and because it put food on the table isn't enough. Fallen humans are so tormented by the empty space inside—the part God should fill—that thcy substitute material acquisition, career prestige, or power for God.
	The resulting failure to fill that space makes humans greedy—they can never get enough (the New Testament word for greed is *pleonexia*—the desire for more). Paul explicitly links greed and idol worship (Colossians 3:5).
Free moral agents	God made humans with the ability to freely think and choose. As we saw earlier, only this makes humans capable of moral or immoral behavior. It also enables us to think rationally and behave in ways not determined by genetics or environment.
	Since the fall, human freedom has been compromised. A clear example is addiction. But impaired freedom goes way beyond substance abuse. Fallen people are subject to all manner of compulsions, obsessions, and habits, often directly against their will.
	All this is the enslaving power of sin, and the damage sin wreaked in our fallen natures.
Relational	Moving self to the center has a catastrophic effect on human relationships. People cannot come together in self-giving love, because their natures are selfish. They come for love-taking. The self-centered, fallen man sizes her up, wondering if she's good enough. She hopes he will complete

	what's empty within her.
	I can spend all evening in the middle of people and go home still lonely. I wasn't able to connect. Why? My relational abilities have been damaged.
	My loved one is sitting right there, why can't I express love? Why am I always dissatisfied with my relationships? Why do I always face abandonment? Why am I so self-protectiv? These and many more are the inevitable consequence of the fall. Negative, abusive experiences make it worse.
Creativity	Paul describes the course of fallen thinking in Romans 1:21-22 "Even though they knew God, they did not honor him as God or give thanks, but they became futile in their speculations, and their foolish heart was darkened. Professing to be wise, they became fools."
	Apart from God, human thinking runs amok. They find it necessary to create answers either apart from God, or with a god of their own making. They end up "suppressing the truth in unrighteousness" (Romans 1:18).
	Fallen thinkers distort their conclusions in a God-proof way. They have no real loyalty to the truth. They often devote their intellectual brilliance to evil goals. A huge proportion of human creativity has been expressed in military innovation.
Sex, unity & diversity	Self-centered lovers have major problems forming union relationships. Pornography, fornication, rape, perversion, and adultery are rampant throughout fallen human history.

	Humans become sexual hunters and manipulators. Marriage and the family suffer. Barriers to union relationships include jealousy, territoriality, and disappointed expectations. They won't be faithful to each other. The first family is a disaster with bitter envy leading to murder. In the millennia to follow, nothing changes. When self moves to the center, humans use each others' bodies for sexual self-gratification, while avoiding commitment. Others are tied up in knots and unable to enjoy sex or respond naturally because of psychological alienation, abuse, and self-protection.
Shameless, uninhibited and free	Fallen people have their eyes on self, and usually don't like what they see. They are ashamed, tied up in themselves, and afraid of the true God. They might be dissatisfied with their bodies, harm themselves, or even commit suicide.

The big picture

Distrust of God led the first humans to fall away from his leadership. The path back to God begins by reversing that distrust to trust. In the Bible, trust is called "faith." When we ask the question, "What does God want from me?" The answer comes back: "faith." "I want you to trust me."

The most amazing part of this story about a race of violent, selfish, lying creatures is this: God still loves us!

Of course, it will take a lot to undo this damage. In Christ we can regain all of the distorted and misshapen features of humanity as God intended—not entirely, but substantially. Then, when we get to heaven, we'll regain them completely.

22 God Hints At His Plan

Genesis 3:14-17

We already noted that God saw all of this coming. Adam and Eve didn't know that at the time. But as the evil one and the humans came before God, he announced the consequences of the fall.

To the serpent

First he addresses the serpent:

> The Lord God said to the serpent, "Because you have done this, cursed are you more than all cattle, and more than every beast of the field; on your belly you will go, and dust you will eat all the days of your life." (Genesis 3:14)

This was not the point at which snakes began slithering on their bellies. Rather, Calvin correctly argues that after the snake had been raised up to an unreal state by Satan, it is now returned ignominiously to his former state.[1] God basically sent the animal back to his hole.

To eat dust suggests the idea of total defeat and groveling before the victor:

> The wolf and the lamb will graze together, and the lion will eat straw like the ox; and dust will be the serpent's food. They will do no evil or harm in all my holy mountain," says the Lord. (Isaiah 65:25; see also Micah 7:17)

---

[1] John Calvin, *Commentary on Genesis*, Chapter 3. We were taught in Sunday school that snakes walked on legs like lizards up to this time, and that vestigial hip bones found in some snakes prove this. While it is true that snakes probably came from a lizard-like ancestor and some have vestigial bones, this transition happened 150-200 million years ago (depending on what source you believe). That was long before humans appeared.

To Satan

To Satan, who animated the serpent, he said,

> And I will put enmity between you and the woman, and between your seed and her seed; he shall bruise you on the head, and you shall bruise him on the heel." (3:15)

This statement is somewhat cryptic, but the enmity between Satan and humans is clear enough. Satan hates human beings, and he always has, because God loves them. Jesus said he was a murderer from the beginning (John 8:44).

Only Satan, the serpent, and the ground are cursed. Although they are punished, neither human is said to be cursed.

The seed of woman

The most mysterious part of this saying is the part about the woman's seed. It's more traditional to speak of the man's seed. Also, her seed is called "he" rather than "they." The seed of Satan bruises her seed on the heel—a painful wound. Her seed bruises Satan on the head—a fatal wound.

It's the first hint of where things are going. The seed of woman is Jesus. At this stage in his plan, God only gave cryptic hints about what he was planning to do.[2]

Later, he gave another, related hint in connection with Moses' bronze serpent. The people were in sin, grumbling against God, and God sent a deadly plague of serpents as a judgment. When Moses interceded for the people, God had him create a bronze serpent and mount it on a pole in the middle of the camp. When they looked to the serpent on the pole, their snakebite would be healed (Numbers 21:6-9).

Jesus referred to this incident, comparing it to the Son of Man being lifted up on the cross, "As Moses lifted up the

---

[2] I suggest a reason why God limits himself to hints in Dennis McCallum, *Satan and his Kingdom*, Chapters 4 and 5.

serpent in the wilderness, even so must the Son of Man be lifted up; so that whoever believes will in him have eternal life" (John 3:14-15).

Why would a serpent be a symbol of Jesus? It's because on the cross, God "Made him who knew no sin to be sin, that we might become the righteousness of God in him" (2 Corinthians 5:21). Peter says, "He Himself bore our sins in His body on the cross, so that we might die to sin and live to righteousness: (1 Peter 2:14). So using a serpent—normally an evil symbol—to stand for Jesus on the cross bearing the sin of humanity, was appropriate.

The virgin birth?

We also have a hint here of Jesus' virgin birth. Perhaps God decided on a virgin birth for Jesus because Satan attacked humanity through the first woman.

Or, it may have been for other reasons. Paul always attributes our fallen nature to Adam, not Eve. Is the fallen nature inherited through the male? If so, Jesus, born of a woman only, would not have had a fallen nature. Instead of having sinful flesh, he would come "*in the likeness of* sinful flesh" (Romans 8:3 emphasis added). We're speculating here on the reason, but not on the fact of the virgin birth.

Eve's seed bruising Satan's head could be what Paul refers to in Romans 16:20: "And the God of peace will crush Satan under your feet shortly" (Rom. 16:20). So our expansion of God's kingdom constantly chips away at the world system—Satan's kingdom. That no doubt adds to his hatred of humans.

To the woman

> To the woman He said, "I will greatly multiply your pain in childbirth, in pain you will bring forth children; yet your desire will be for your husband, and he will rule over you."

God isn't saying he wants men to rule over women, or that he wants women to suffer in childbirth. He is saying these things are going to happen as a result of humans throwing off his protection and leadership. They are the natural outcome of human autonomy.

Passive judgment

These so-called "curses" are really more like pronouncements. God is not saying these are his will for us, but that we brought these consequences on ourselves. Most of them are describing "passive judgment." In passive judgment, God only has to do nothing for the judgment to occur. But it's still judgment, because he could have prevented it.

For instance, in the next pronouncement he predicts the earth will bring forth thorns and thistles. That doesn't mean God points his finger and creates thorns and thistles. He is simply saying he won't protect us from the negative aspects of nature, unlike what would have happened if we never fell.

Here, too, God's pronouncements toward Eve are describing some of the unfortunate things that can be expected now that humans have gone away from his leadership and onto their own.

Physical pain

You see the importance of understanding the nature of passive judgment in the increased pain women can expect during childbirth. Should we avoid using painkillers during delivery in order to make sure women feel as much pain as possible? No! This pain is a misfortune that should be mitigated, just as we wouldn't hesitate to pull thorns and thistles out of a garden.

Bondage to men

So too, with the declaration about women being needy and subservient to their men. Some interpreters argue that this decree establishes husbands as leaders in the home. But if so, why is it listed as one of the curses or negative consequences of their sin?

It seems more likely that this declaration predicts that males will use women's natural desire for a husband and family as a way to manipulate them and dominate them. It's not God's will. It's his warning that this is going to be the tendency. And it has come true in spades. Male domination of females has been one of the most over-arching themes in history.

The fact that men exploit and abuse women is not God's will; it's evil. God was not suggesting that husbands *should* rule over their wives, only that they will. People are now selfish, and men tend to be physically larger than women. Those facts, put together, make domination of women inevitable.

The New Testament calls on wives to submit to their husbands' leadership, but that's referring to servant leadership. Servant leadership envisages godly, humble men who are leaders willing to sacrifice themselves for their wives' good, just like Jesus loved the church and gave himself up for her (Ephesians 5:25).

They view their wives as being as valuable as their own bodies, and "nourish and cherish them" (Ephesians 5:22-33). It does not show husbands "ruling over" their wives as in this dark passage. The desire to rule over others is the spirit of the Gentiles, that Jesus denounced (Mark 10:42).

To the man

> Then to Adam He said, "Because you have listened to the voice of your wife,[3] and have eaten from the tree about which I commanded you, saying, 'You shall

---

[3] This clause argues against the notion that Adam was actually standing there when the serpent tempted Eve. If that were the case, God would have said, "Because you listened to the voice of the serpent...." This says Adam got the suggestion to eat from Eve. The passage's smack down on passive males stands just as strong either way.

> not eat from it'; cursed is the ground because of you;
> in toil you will eat of it all the days of your life. Both
> thorns and thistles it shall grow for you; and you will
> eat the plants of the field; by the sweat of your face
> you will eat bread, till you return to the ground,
> because from it you were taken; for you are dust,
> and to dust you shall return." (Genesis 3:17-19)

This pronouncement includes a curse on the ground. God's curse on the ground suggests that it will yield food grudgingly. The presence of unwanted thorns and thistles suggests that other unwanted organisms will also cause problems.

This was not the time at which weeds, pathogenic bacteria, viruses, and nasty insects appeared. Those go back many millions of years. Rather, it was again the point when humans lost God's protection from negative organisms. This is also when we lost God's protection from earthquakes, volcanoes, hurricanes, floods, and other natural disasters.

The principle here is that humans can't have it both ways. If they had followed God, he would have protected them (and us) from these dangers. But people can't throw off God's leadership and still expect to benefit from his protection. A decision to go it alone is a decision to go it alone. And being apart from God is a dangerous and difficult place to be.

This explains what's wrong with our world today and throughout history.

Here too is the decree that people will die physically. This is probably part and parcel of the same point above. Ageing is not necessary in theory, but probably requires protection from genetic damage, harmful mutations, cosmic radiation, dangerous microbes, and other causes of death.

Not spiritualism

Some readers go astray here. They think everything bad that happens is the result of divine judgment, and therefore causation. If a tsunami strikes, it's because God was angry at those people. And they base that view in part on this passage.

The result is a worldview called "theistic determinism" or, a related worldview known as "animism." Under either of these views, the one and only cause of everything that happens in the world is the action of spirit beings—either the God of monotheism or lesser gods or spirits in nature.

As we argued earlier, neither of these views matches the biblical worldview. Jesus asked, "Do you suppose that those eighteen on whom the tower in Siloam fell and killed them were worse culprits than all the men who live in Jerusalem?" (Luke 13:4). To his hearers in the rabbinic Jewish tradition, the answer would be, "Well, they died, and I'm sure God wouldn't do anything unfair... so yes! They must have deserved it."

But Jesus rejected their view: "I tell you, no, but unless you repent, you will all likewise perish" (v. 5). The reason the tower killed those people was not because they were worse sinners. It was because they were standing under where the tower fell. No further explanation is needed, and it would be arrogant to supply one.

Cause and effect operate all around us, based on the system of physics and chemistry God created. In addition, God may intervene to alter the direction of cause and effect as he wills. But he may let the cause and effect sequence continue without intervening most of the time. In those cases, he could still state that the outcome is a judgment from him, because he could have intervened but did not.

So God may directly cause something, or he may let things happen based on physical cause and effect or human free choice, and other incidents could be the action of Satan. To claim otherwise—that everything is caused by God for reasons of justice—is the same false view advanced by Job's friends in the book of Job. God rebuked them and took offense that they claimed to know what he was doing and why (Job 38:2; 42:7-9).[4] Such claims are arrogant and unwarranted. Many, and probably most of the tragedies we see in the fallen world are the result of natural cause and effect.

Because the world is fallen, we can expect negative events and natural tragedies to burst upon the scene regularly. Notice God's words, "Both thorns and thistles it shall grow for you." The "it" here is the earth. The earth itself produces thorns and thistles without any need for God to intervene. The same goes for earthquakes, storms, and disease. The sad fact is that it didn't have to be this way.

Clothing

> The Lord God made garments of skin for Adam and his wife, and clothed them. (Genesis 3:21)

Here is God's alternative to their fig leaves. Instead of coming from their imagination, these coverings came from God. To provide them, one or more animals must have died. You could say the animals gave their lives to cover the humans.

Would we be stretching it to see here an early example of animal substitutionary death? Maybe. But I think probably not. We see that they taught their sons, Cain and Abel to offer sacrifices to God, so they must have learned that somewhere. The important point is that the covering comes from God.

---

[4] An example of the foolish and blind worldview that angered God is that of Eliphaz. He says, "Who ever perished being innocent? Or where were the upright destroyed? According to what I have seen, those who plow iniquity and those who sow trouble harvest it" (Job 4:8-9). So the holocaust happened because they deserved it? No! Christians should always avoid attributing things to God when we don't know and cannot know if that's true. God was so upset at Job's friends he wouldn't talk to them. He made them go to Job and have him intercede (42:7-9).

> Then the Lord God said, "Behold, the man has become like one of Us, knowing good and evil; and now, he might stretch out his hand, and take also from the tree of life, and eat, and live forever"— therefore the Lord God sent him out from the garden of Eden, to cultivate the ground from which he was taken.
>
> So He drove the man out; and at the east of the garden of Eden He stationed the cherubim and the flaming sword which turned every direction to guard the way to the tree of life. (Genesis 3:22-24)

We studied this passage earlier when considering the names of the two trees. Here again, with the cherubim (angels) and the flaming sword, it becomes clear that having eternal life with God is not compatible with autonomy. People must give up their autonomy and come under his leadership before they can receive God's gift.

The big picture

The first humans wandered off "east of Eden." In other words, away from Eden. They have clothes from God, and we must assume, some instructions. But it's a sad picture seeing these two walking off from the life they could have had.

23 The First Family

Genesis 4

Adam knew Eve

> Now the man had relations with his wife Eve, and
> she conceived and gave birth to Cain, and she said,
> "I have gotten a manchild with the help of the Lord."
> (Genesis 4:1)

As the first family is banished from Eden and from the tree
of eternal life, all is not lost. What an astonishing
experience it must have been for the first couple to be
pregnant and deliver a child! Eve correctly concluded that
the new child was of God. He alone could create a new soul.

> Now Abel kept flocks, and Cain worked the soil. In
> the course of time Cain brought some of the fruits of
> the soil as an offering to the Lord. But Abel brought
> fat portions from some of the firstborn of his flock.
> (Genesis 4:2-4)

Cain grew up as a farmer, like his father. His younger
brother, Able, grew up as a shepherd. Both roles were good
and there is no hint in this story that God has a problem
with either.

Back in the day, we were taught that Abel offered a good
sacrifice because it was a blood offering for atonement.
Symbolically, one's sins were transferred onto the innocent
animal, and then the animal died instead of the sinner.

Cain, according to this teaching erred because he offered
the fruit of his labor, suggesting coming to God based on
his own works.

That explanation is wrong. First, grain offerings and drink
offerings were common in the Old Testament, and signified

thanksgiving for the harvest. Abel's offering is also probably a thank offering, because it's only the fat portions.

The real issue is right there to the careful reader in verse 5: "The Lord looked with favor on Abel and his offering, but on Cain and his offering he did not look with favor." It was "Abel and his offering."

God looks on the heart to see where someone stands with him. As he later explained to Samuel, "The Lord doesn't see things the way you see them. People judge by outward appearance, but the Lord looks at the heart" (1 Samuel 16:7). Through Isaiah he said, "These people say they are mine. They honor me with their lips, but their hearts are far from me. And their worship of me is nothing but man-made rules learned by rote." (Isaiah 29:13).

Outward religious performance means nothing to God. He looks through all the outward right deep into the heart. And as the subsequent story shows, he was not mistaken about Cain's darkened heart.

Something about Abel, on the other hand caused God to look upon him with favor. We learn what it is in Hebrews 11:4: "By faith Abel offered God a better sacrifice than Cain did. By faith he was commended as a righteous man, when God spoke well of his offerings. And by faith he still speaks, even though he is dead." Abel had the one thing God asks of us—trust, or faith. That's why God looked upon him with favor.

Cain's heart

If Abel was accepted because of his faith, we can surmise that Cain did not come to God based on faith. Therefore, he must have come to God based on the alternative to faith— his own works. So the old timers were right on one thing— that it was faith versus works at stake here. But it wasn't the offerings that were good or bad, it was the men themselves.

When we think about Cain, we can see he believed God existed because he's making an offering. Objectively, he performed a religious ritual connected with the God of the Bible. But this kind of religiosity could be not only worthless but sinful. Cain's problem is that he came on his own terms, not on God's terms.

Many make the same mistake today. They think being good or doing some rituals satisfies God. But God can't accept this approach. At the root of this approach is pride. People assume then and today that they can earn God's favor. But that's never possible. Only the second Adam could secure God's acceptance for sinful humans.

God somehow let Cain know, "No, Cain, I can't accept that."

The psychology of sin

This story is not primarily about murder. It's about the process of a heart sliding away from God. We read, "So Cain was very angry, and his face was downcast" (v. 5). Poor Cain! No, wait. He has nothing to be angry about. Anger here signals a bad, rebellious attitude.

Self-pity is like a thermometer for unbelief. The more we pity ourselves, the less we are trusting God. In fact, Cain was probably reproaching God in his heart for blessing someone else. He was self-righteous. Jealous.

Cain should have been humbly pleading with God for instruction and help, to understand what the problem was, and how he could overcome it. His anger suggests he felt he deserved better. And then, there's the comparison with Abel. When your eyes come off of God and onto comparing yourself with others, that's when you begin to envy and feel like you got a raw deal. God immediately knew what his anger meant.

> Then the Lord said to Cain, "Why are you angry? And why has your countenance fallen? If you do well, will not your countenance be lifted up? And if you do not

do well, sin is crouching at the door; and its desire is for you, but you must master it." (vs. 6-7)

God points Cain to the truth: He hasn't been messed over at all. (Strange that God forgot to validate Cain's feelings!) His only problem is with himself. This sin crouching at the door is not external to Cain. It's his own sin within. Before Cain are two paths: either "do well" or allow his mind to become the plaything of sin and the evil one.

What does it mean to do well? God doesn't say. That's because he has no reason to go into details with Cain when the central question is whether he's willing. It's pointless to fuss with steps and specifics with someone who is fundamentally unwilling.

God's provision for temptation

What it means to "do well" depends. For each willing believer in each situation, God will give what Paul calls, "a way of escape,"

> No temptation has overtaken you but such as is common to man; and God is faithful, who will not allow you to be tempted beyond what you are able, but with the temptation will provide the way of escape also, so that you will be able to endure it.
> (1 Corinthians 10:13)

In this important promise—really no different than what God was saying to Cain—the danger is implied. Paul's readers must have also felt like they were being treated unfairly; that God hadn't come through; that it was just too hard. In the muddled thinking engendered by unbelief, one can easily become angry at God for putting him or her into an untenable situation.

Those in a healthy faith relationship with God know he has not abandoned them. God has them in this situation, and he reveals something they can do. It varies widely. Go open up to a mature believer you know? Read that book specifically about your problem? Admit your problem honestly to a friend? Add some accountability software to you computer and phone? Pray along these lines?

Notice that the "way of escape" doesn't mean the trial will stop. Rather, it's "so that you will be able to endure it." So what are you escaping? You're escaping the downhill logic of unbelief that can reach out and claim your mind. Just as God warned Cain, "sin is crouching at the door, and its desire is for you." How evocative! Is it an exaggeration?

No. This is exactly how to view it. You fall into sin. God confronts you with discipline. Now, you either humble yourself, run to God, and gain his shelter. Or your pride wells up, you become sullen, you don't want to look at God and you feel sorry for yourself. Discipline is never easy to accept, but we need it in the worst way.

Cain failed

> Now Cain said to his brother Abel, "Let's go out to the field." And while they were in the field, Cain attacked his brother Abel and killed him. (v. 7)

It seems incredibly extreme. But when someone enters into the sequence of hardening his or her heart, anything is possible. You might find yourself doing things you never would have believed possible. That's especially true when your mind is poisoned with bitterness and jealousy.

But killing Abel failed to solve Cain's problem. He could do away with the irritant of the moment, but he couldn't run away from his own bitter heart.

Accountability

> Then the Lord said to Cain, "Where is your brother Abel?"
> "I don't know," he replied. "Am I my brother's keeper?"
> The Lord said, "What have you done? Listen! Your brother's blood cries out to me from the ground."
> (vs. 9-10)

Coarse, tough, dishonest, and heartless—isn't it amazing that Cain didn't burst into tears before God? Cain's sin had been chaffing against his conscience so hard he had developed a thick layer of callous over his heart.

Cain still could have repented. This text isn't teaching that Cain had gone too far for God. That's why God asked him where his brother was. He was giving Cain a chance to confess and plead for mercy. What had gone too far was Cain's hardening of his own heart. The psychology of sin dictates strong measures to suppress guilt feelings.

Dishonesty and sin

Cain is a liar, and his lies are designed to avoid admitting his sin. Just like his father, hiding behind a tree, Cain is lying and dodging to avoid admitting his fault. He didn't trust God's grace enough to run to him, pleading for forgiveness.

The simple lie Cain could have told in response to God's question is, "I don't know." Why add the comment, "Am I my brother's keeper?" Is he being sarcastic? Is it to throw God off the track? Is he unable to conceal his contempt? Is he layering lies, hoping to be more persuasive? It seems like a sneering retort to God, implying God's question is unreasonable. This counter question from Cain definitely didn't come with a smile.

In history, Cain's dodge has become proverbial. "Am I my brother's keeper?" is often used humorously today, minus the awful fact that he had just murdered Abel.

God cursed Cain.

> Now you are cursed from the ground, which has opened its mouth to receive your brother's blood from your hand. When you work the ground, it will no longer yield its crops for you. You will be a restless wanderer on the earth. (vs. 11-12)

Irony is here—because Cain misused the ground and stained it with the blood of his brother, the ground would no longer respond to his efforts to farm. In addition he was exiled from his own family, which he had now shattered.

Marks of an unrepentant heart

> Cain said to the Lord, "My punishment is more than I can bear. Today you are driving me from the land, and I will be hidden from your presence; I will be a restless wanderer on the earth, and whoever finds me will kill me." (vs. 13-14)

The clear signs of an unrepentant heart are here. First, he can't understand why he should suffer serious consequences, just because he murdered his brother. He continues to think he's being treated unfairly, even though this sentence is actually surprisingly mild compared to what he would have gotten under the law of Moses—death.

Also, all his focus is on self. He's still awash in self-pity. His collapse to lamentation isn't because of Abel, or his parents, who just lost their son—no consciousness of the damage done to others—specifically murder. His whining tone is a sure giveaway that he's unrepentant. He has no appreciation of the enormity of what he's done, and no comprehension of the grace of God.

> But the Lord said to him, "Not so; if anyone kills Cain, he will suffer vengeance seven times over." Then the Lord put a mark on Cain so that no one who found him would kill him. (v. 15)

We don't know what Cain's mark was—maybe people were just scared by him. But it's clearly an act of grace from God.

The big picture

And so, the very sad epithet comes:

> So Cain went out from the Lord's presence and lived in the land of Nod, east of Eden. (v. 16)

There goes the crown prince of the human race—out from God's presence. Nod means "to wander."

So right in the first family we have murder. And murder has been one of the greatest themes of history—not only by individuals, but by families, gangs, tribes, and finally the ultimate slayers, nation states. Nations can coordinate hundreds of thousands for humankind's most fearful pastime: warfare.

Nations have worked on improving their ability to war over the centuries up until the twentieth century—the ultimate century for slaughter. By the end of the century it is estimated that just in that century, more than 150 million died in battle and war-caused civilian deaths. Another 50 million or more died from ethnic cleansing or communist genocides. That would have matched the entire population of Earth, men, women, and children, at the time of the New Testament.

Already with Cain, the well known features of the psychology of sin are all evident. Because Cain was unrepentant, his sin drove him away from God and from the people of God. He couldn't face the truth about himself, and so blamed his problems on others—especially God.

Already man-made, phony religion rears its head. Cain was going through the motions of offering a thank offering, but events soon revealed what God knew all along—that Cain's heart was as far from God as it could be; that his religious act was nothing but a sham. The act of coming before God with hate in your heart is something Jesus described as totally unacceptable (Matthew 5:23-24).

24 Antediluvian History

Genesis 5

an(t)ēdə'loōvēən - before the biblical flood

The line of Cain

After the murder, "Cain went out from the presence of the Lord" (Genesis 4:16). Now people were out wandering around, doing their own thing.

Where would Cain find a wife? Notice that Adam and Eve were long lived, and fertile. See Genesis 4:4 "Then the days of Adam after he became the father of Seth were eight hundred years, and he had other sons and daughters." The same goes for the other people in the genealogies. We can imagine very many offspring in this period, and Cain married one of them.

We see two features in the line of Cain.

Advancement

People in the line of Cain in Genesis 4 get busy immediately excelling in technology and culture:

- v. 17 Enoch builds the first city, and then names it after himself. City life and the civilization that goes with it (like writing) only go back to about 4000 BC.

- v. 20 Jabal establishes agriculture. Again, anthropologists believe cultivating annual crops only goes back to 8 to 12 thousand years.

- v. 21 His brother, Jubal is given credit for advancing music and the arts through making instruments.

- v. 22 Attributes metallurgy to Tubal-cain. Any iron work at this time would have been meteoric iron.

So this line of descendents is rapidly developing features associated with civilization. However, there are negatives as well.[1]

- v. 19 Lamech marries two wives, thus departing from the pattern God had established in Genesis 2—that the two become one. This is the first mention of polygamy.

- vs. 23-24 Discuss Lamech's attitude: And Lamech said to his wives, "Adah and Zillah, Listen to my voice, You wives of Lamech, Give heed to my speech, For I have killed a man for wounding me; And a boy for striking me; If Cain is avenged sevenfold, Then Lamech seventy-sevenfold."

Here is the pride, swagger, and violence that the great ones in history exhibit. Being tougher, more ruthless, and more powerful than others has become a key to establish one's identity apart from God.

The line of Seth

Meanwhile, the line of Seth is unremarkable. The writer only pauses to make two comments:

4:26 "Then men began to call upon the name of the Lord."

5:22 "Then Enoch walked with God...."

So this comparison and contrast is clearly deliberate for the author. He is suggesting the emergence of two humanities. One is rich in materialistic, cultural, and technological progress, and at the same time it manifests ruthless, violent self-advancement.

The other humanity is materially unremarkable, but has an interest in spiritual things. They probably made

---

[1] Some of these skills could have been around earlier if there were lines of hominids who became extinct, as claimed in the "gap theory" of creation. Under that view, this is a restart, not necessarily the first instance.

advancements in the other areas as well, but that's not what stands out. Wise people understand putting God first.

You can see the wisdom in living for God through the refrain of these genealogies. The pattern is, "he lived...he did this or that... and he died." The poignancy and the futility stand out.

What's the point of building a city or fashioning metal when your death instantly cancels out everything you did? How many of us have spent a vacation in the city of Enoch? Where is this land of Nod? These texts are artifacts of a world swept away by death.

Death is abnormal for humans. It's not part of God's will. Paul says in 1 Corinthians 15:25-26, "For He must reign until He has put all His enemies under His feet. The last enemy that will be abolished is death." So Jesus views death as his enemy, as something he is out to destroy.

Then, later, God throws death into the lake of fire, along with Satan (Revelation 20:14). These genealogies ring in the sad outcome of an undeniable fact that, "In Adam all die" (1 Corinthians 15:22). But we shouldn't miss the rest of the verse: "so also in Christ all will be made alive."

As followers, our lives are not swept away, especially when we invest into eternal things, like our believing friends and family, who are going to be there with us.

Adam's heritage

Although Seth's line was apparently more spiritual, they too could only have what they were given. We read,

> This is the book of the generations of Adam. In the day when God created man, He made him in the likeness of God. He created them male and female, and He blessed them and named them Man in the day when they were created.
>
> When Adam had lived one hundred and thirty years, he became the father of a son in his own likeness,

> according to his image, and named him Seth.
> (Genesis 5:1-3)

So Adam was created in God's image, but Seth? He was created in Adam's image. Adam's fallen nature was passed to his child. Adam was given the power to give life. But now he gave rise to fallen children who were in his image.

Minimum time span

While the ages in these genealogies are huge, they also apparently overlap. You can see this in the typical example of Kenan:

> Kenan lived seventy years, and became the father of Mahalalel. Then Kenan lived eight hundred and forty years after he became the father of Mahalalel, and he had other sons and daughters. So all the days of Kenan were nine hundred and ten years, and he died." (Genesis 5:12-14)

So Kenan was seventy years old when he had Mahalalel. That's the true distance between generations, not nine hundred plus years.

Adding all these smaller time spans together results in a minimum (not maximum) span of less than seventeen hundred years between Adam and the flood. If so, it becomes much easier to imagine all humans still living in the fertile crescent at the time of the flood. This is what many local flood readers suggest.

Maximum time span

For any author of a genealogy in the modern world, skipping generations would be unthinkable, but not in antiquity. We know for a fact that genealogies in the Bible do sometimes omit generations. This is because the purpose of the genealogy is to show direction of descent, not length of time.

You see this in the genealogy from Levi to Moses given in Exodus 6:16-20. There, Moses was the great grandson of

Levi through his father, Amram. But the Kohathites, made up of Amram and his brothers' families, numbered 8,600 males in Moses' day (Numbers 3:28).

So Amram must have lived long before this time, or the term "Amram" means "the family of Amram." And of course, we know Levi had been dead for four hundred years at the time of Moses, so there's no way three generations could span that length of time.[2]

You see the same thing in the New Testament, where Matthew's genealogy for Jesus leaves out six or seven Old Testament figures. The reason comes at the end of the list:

> So all the generations from Abraham to David are fourteen generations; from David to the deportation to Babylon, fourteen generations; and from the deportation to Babylon to the Messiah, fourteen generations. (Matthew 1:17)

Matthew wanted each section to come out to the number 14. Ancient authors did this for memory purposes. People actually memorized their lineage or that of other great ones. This way, the student could check himself by counting how many he recited, and having it come out to fourteen for each section.

Hebrew usage also sometimes says grandfathers or grandmothers had begotten their grandsons (e.g., Bilhah's grandsons are spoken of as her sons in 1 Chronicles 7:13).

So here, in Genesis 4 and 5, we could also have missing generations. The expression, "Seth became the father of Enosh" can mean "Seth became the ancestor of Enosh," or "Seth fathered the line of Enosh."

One reason for suspecting missing generations here is that, in a pattern similar to Matthew's, we see a grouping into

---

[2] Again, Exodus 6:14-25 presents four generations from Levi to Moses, but 1 Chronicles 7:23-27 presents a more realistic ten generations to cover the same period. Ezra 7:1-5 omits six names that are given in 1 Chronicles 6:3-14. So we can rest assured that ancient Hebrew practice included selective inclusion in these lists.

ten pre-flood and ten post-flood generations. That would be quite a coincidence. Or, much more likely, it was intentional.

So, scholars have suggested that this genealogy could extend for thousands of years. That's possible, but it's doubtful that there are many more generations than those listed. It won't stretch out to 200,000 years to match up with secular anthropology's date for the beginning of homo sapiens. Even the fifty thousand years for early modern Homo Sapiens would be a stretch.

The big picture

Between Adam and the flood, the human race probably multiplied rapidly. With people living to great age (more on this later), they could have many offspring. The ones mentioned here are just selections from the total. Depending on whether the longer interval or the shorter one is right, there were probably anywhere from thousands to millions of humans by the time of Chapter 6.

While a small minority may have been following God, the overwhelming majority were busy building their cities and fighting with each other. The negatives were building up to the point where God had to act.

25 The Genesis Flood: Critical Issues

History came to a climax of evil. God was unwilling to let things continue in this direction. He declared,

> The end of all flesh has come before me; for the earth is filled with violence because of them; and behold, I am about to destroy them with the earth. (Genesis 6:14)

Before going into the story, we need to think through several issues:

1. Occult sexuality and the *Nephilim*
2. God's grief for creating humans
3. Universal or local flood?
4. The virtual destruction of the human race
5. Other flood stories

Occult sexuality?

> When men began to increase in number on the earth and daughters were born to them, the sons of God saw that the daughters of men were beautiful, and they married any of them they chose. Then the Lord said, "My Spirit will not contend with man forever, for he is mortal; his days will be a hundred and twenty years."
> The Nephilim were on the earth in those days—and also afterward—when the sons of God went to the daughters of men and had children by them. They were the heroes of old, men of renown. (Genesis 6:1-4)

This passage advances the far out claim that "the sons of God went to the daughters of men and had children by them," resulting in offspring called "*Nephilim.*" The King James translates *Nephilim* as "giants": "There were giants in the earth in those days."

What are the "sons of God"?

Ancient readers took the "sons of God" to be angels. The term, "sons of God" is used to refer to angels in Job 38:7. This view emerged clearly during the inter-testamental period (between Malachi and Matthew) especially in the non-canonical books having to do with Enoch.[1]

Aside from the pre-Christian sources, Jude 6-7 says,

> And angels who did not keep their own domain, but abandoned their proper abode, He has kept in eternal bonds under darkness for the judgment of the great day, just as Sodom and Gomorrah and the cities around them, since they in the same way as these indulged in gross immorality and went after strange flesh, are exhibited as an example in undergoing the punishment of eternal fire.

Are the angels here the same as the "sons of God" in Genesis 6? By comparing with Peter's statement, it seems that they are. He connects the angels sent to pits of darkness with the time of Noah:

> For if God did not spare angels when they sinned, but cast them into hell and committed them to pits of darkness, reserved for judgment; and did not spare the ancient world, but preserved Noah, a preacher of righteousness, with seven others, when He brought a flood upon the world of the ungodly. (2 Peter 2:4-5)

---

[1] All early sources refer to the "sons of heaven" as angels, from the third century BC. onwards. In addition to the Enoch related literature, we see the same view in the Dead Sea Scrolls (the *Genesis Apocryphon*, the *Damascus Document*, 4Q180), *Jubilees*, the *Testament of Reuben*, *2 Baruch*, and Josephus, *Antiquities of the Jews*, 1: 3, 1.

The plain sense reading of these two passages suggests that these "sons of God" in Genesis 6 were, in fact, angels who "went after strange flesh." That would suggest angelic beings mating successfully with human women to produce hybrid offspring of some kind.

In assessing this view, remember that the term "angel" means "messenger," and is apparently a broad term. It refers to multiple different kinds of creatures. In the Old Testament we read of cherubim, seraphim, archangels, and other angels. These are different kinds of creatures.

Paul refers to "rulers," "powers," "world forces of this darkness," and "spiritual forces of wickedness," all apparently referring to different kinds of angels. He also says our struggle is not with "flesh and blood" (Ephesians 6:12), so none of the creatures he mentions had flesh in their makeup. On the other hand, later in Genesis two angels went to Lot's house, "and they ate"(Genesis 19:3). They also ate and drank with Abraham in Chapter 18. So angels interact with matter, like when they rolled the stone away from Jesus' tomb.

But other creatures of a more physical nature (like humans, who combine the physical and the spiritual) might have existed at one time, and they could have been called "angels" or "sons of God." If so, Jude says they are no longer around, because they have been imprisoned. Peter agrees that God, "cast them into hell and committed them to pits of darkness."

So these are not creatures we need to worry about any more. According to this reading, these are a type of creature we have never seen.

An alternative view

Many commentators think the "sons of God" here are not angels, but humans from the line of Seth who married women from the line of Cain.

This view took root in post-New Testament times in both Christian and Jewish sources.[2]

Orthodox Judaism has taken a stance against the idea that Genesis 6 refers to angels or that angels could intermarry with men. Shimon bar Yochai pronounced a curse on anyone teaching this idea. Rashi and Nachmanides followed this. All these sources are post-Christian.

Some individuals and groups, including Augustine, John Chrysostom, and John Calvin, agree with the view that the sons of God are humans from the line of Cain.

The view is not without difficulty, considering the passages cited earlier from Jude and 2 Peter. Also, if these were normal humans, why were their offspring "the mighty men of old, men of renown"? In fact, why would something so unremarkable even come up in the context of why God drew the line and sent a flood? This cross breeding of some kind comes up here because it is typical of the moral disintegration at that time, leading to the flood (v. 6:5).

What are the Nephilim?

The offspring of these unions are called "*Nephilim*." Moses also describes them as "the heroes of old, men of renown." Readers of religious and occult mythology will quickly recognize this common theme of a god or demon mating with a human female. Think of Hercules or Achilles for example, who were both said to be of half-human, half-god parentage.

Nephilim come up again in Numbers 13:32–33, where the spies reported on the promised land:

> The land through which we have gone, in spying it out, is a land that devours its inhabitants; and all the people whom we saw in it are men of great size. There also we saw the Nephilim (the sons of Anak are

---

[2] Sources who hold this include Rabbi Shimon bar Yochai, Augustine of Hippo, Sextus, Julius Africanus, and both letters of Clement.

part of the Nephilim); and we became like grasshoppers in our own sight, and so we were in their sight.

So this passage suggests that *Nephilim* is a term for warriors of great size. The original Hebrew stem means "to fall." Perhaps "to fall upon a prey" (therefore, warriors?) or "the fallen ones" (associated with fallen angels?).

The Septuagint translated it with the Greek *gigantes* or giants, and the Latin Vulgate and King James followed that reading.[3]

Inter-testamental apocryphal books took up the account in Genesis 6 with zeal and lurid fascination. They consistently portray it as angels and humans producing supernatural offspring, including giants.[4]

Of course, the idea of a giant is relative. Goliath is considered a giant, and according to important variant readings, may have been only six feet, six inches tall.[5] That would still be gigantic at a time when the average man was barely over five feet tall.

The Book of Jubilees (7:21–25) states that ridding the Earth of these *Nephilim* was one of God's purposes for flooding the Earth in Noah's time. You get a hint of this in our modern translations of Genesis 6.

---

[3] Other ancient versions following the "giants" translation include the *Theodotion*, the *Samaritan Targum, Targum Onkelos*, and *Targum Neofiti*. These are all later than the first century AD.

[4] The literature connected with Enoch, the Dead Sea Scrolls (the Genesis *Apocryphon*, the *Damascus Document*, 4Q180), *Jubilees*, the *Testament of Reuben*, *2 Baruch*, and Josephus all talk about angels and giants, In *1 Enoch*, they were "great giants, whose height was three thousand ells." An Ell being 18 inches, this would make them 4500 feet (nearly a mile) tall! https://en.wikipedia.org/wiki/Nephilim.

[5] 1 Samuel 17:4 *Holman Christian Standard Bible* (HCSB), Footnote 1. "DSS [Dead Sea Scrolls], LXX [Septuagint – Greek translation of the OT] read four cubits and a span." That would be a much less problematic height of 6'6", rather than 9'6". These two important sources are independent from each other, and therefore carry more weight versus the Masoretic text.

Extreme evil

The heart of the message in the run up to the flood is humanity's obsession and thirst for evil at this time. Genesis 6:5 says, "Then the Lord saw that the wickedness of man was great on the earth, and that every intent of the thoughts of his heart was only evil continually."

At this point in history, the text says, "Noah was a righteous man, the only blameless person living on earth at the time, and he walked in close fellowship with God" (6:9). What a wonderful description of a man of God! And yet how awful because he was the only one.

This have been a trajectory that would have eliminated following God from the earth. It reads like Noah and his family might have been the last believers in existence. Godly living was on life support.

God's grief

> The Lord was grieved that he had made man on the earth, and his heart was filled with pain. (Genesis 6:6)

This verse is problematic because it makes it sound like God was shocked and saddened, and that he realized making humans was a big mistake.

But we know God is omniscient, and doesn't make mistakes, so he saw this coming even before creation. Neither is this a case of God changing his mind.

Rather, this verse is saying that the low state of humanity caused God emotional sorrow. God is a personal being, not a big brain in a jar, or a gas permeating the universe. And it should be a comfort to us that even in the face of judgment, God feels sorrow.

This theme comes up in other passages as well.

> "Do I have any pleasure in the death of the wicked," declares the Lord God, "rather than that he should

turn from his ways and live?" (Ezekiel 18:23; also 18:32; 33:11)

For he does not afflict willingly or grieve the sons of men. (Lamentations 3:33)

How can I give you up, O Ephraim? How can I surrender you, O Israel? How can I make you like Admah? How can I treat you like Zeboiim? My heart is turned over within Me, All my compassions are kindled. (Hosea 11:8)

The Lord is not slow about his promise, as some count slowness, but is patient toward you, not wishing for any to perish but for all to come to repentance. (2 Peter 3:9)

God our savior, who desires all men to be saved and to come to the knowledge of the truth. (1 Timothy 2:4)

In these and other passages, we sense God weeping in sorrow over judgment—something Jesus literally did, for instance, when he wept over unrepentant Jerusalem (Matthew 23:37; compare with Luke 19:41).

All these passages make it clear that, while God will judge, he is very reluctant to do so, and it hurts his feelings. Judgment comes in when all else has failed. Think how zealous God must be to avoid judging people that he went to the cross!

With the flood, God knew that only radical surgery could save the human race.

Fallen people hate the message of God's judgment, and many of them hate God for even suggesting such a thing. But it isn't up to a vote. An immoral universe without justice would be an abomination. And a God who created moral freedom but doesn't exercise justice would be equally awful. But that's not the way God is. He has the attribute of justice, and he exercises justice as his righteous character dictates.

The scope of the flood

Although most conservative instructors teach a world flood with the waters topping even the Himalayas, others disagree. The biblical and scientific evidence can be read in more than one way.

When reading Genesis 6-8, the language could be understood to mean the flood only covered the area of the Fertile Crescent—a low-lying area.

This is possible because in most cases, the word for "earth" in this account is *eretz*, which can mean "land" rather than "earth." In fact, it's translated "land" at least twice as often as "earth" so this is not an obscure, rare translation. It's the majority translation.

The same goes for the other word, *adamah*, usually translated "ground," but also "land," like in 6:7 "The Lord said, "I will blot out man whom I have created from the face of the land (*adamah*)...." The usual translations for *adamah* are "land(s)" 125 times, "earth" 53 times, "ground" 43 times.[6] So again, the majority meaning is not "earth."

There is another term, *tebel,* which means the whole expanse of the earth, or the world as a whole. But nowhere does *tebel* occur in this account.

Difficulties with a local flood

However, there are problems. To cover even Mesopotamia would require an increase of several hundred feet in sea level. That would, in turn, flood much of the rest of the earth. Some readers think it could have been linked to the end of the last ice age, about 10,000 BC. (which did raise sea level by hundreds of feet). Others have suggested that the continental plate was depressed downward in a major seismic event, causing the ocean waters to inundate the

---

[6] James Strong, *The Exhaustive Concordance of the Bible,* electronic ed., (Ontario: Woodside Bible Fellowship., 1996). H127.

land. Then, an uplift of the plate causing the water to run off.

Another possibility would include God blocking the draining rivers, Tigris and Euphrates, like he did the Jordan River later (Joshua 3). There, the water backed up; it wasn't de-materialized.

Opponents of this view point out that the flood also covered all the hills or mountains "which were under all the heavens." This last phrase suggests it's not just local, but universal. Local Flood readers simply say the sky here is relative to the land in question, just as in Deuteronomy 2:25. "This day I will begin to put the dread and fear of you upon the peoples everywhere under the heavens."

It's really referring to the "heavens" over the nations before them in the land of Canaan. Most nations on earth at the time had no knowledge of the Israelites. Such language is common in many Old Testament passages.

Problems with a universal flood

Modern readers see significant biological problems with a universal flood.

1. If saltwater covered the Earth, how can there still be freshwater lakes?

2. How would animals like the kangaroo have repopulated Australia, but not anywhere else?

3. How could fresh water fish have survived a global flood?

4. How could coral have survived, when they are highly sensitive to an absence of sunlight and to temperature?

5. Many animals have to migrate (e.g., penguins). Others have special diets that could not be transported, and many need a special climate to survive (e.g., polar bears).

6. What did the carnivores eat once they got off of the Ark? If they ate the other species, wouldn't the prey go immediately extinct? What did they eat while on the ark?[7]

Psalm 104

In Psalm 104 the psalmist writes of the glory of creation. He starts out talking about the watery chaos in Genesis 1:1-2:

> He set the earth on its foundations; it can never be moved. You covered it with the deep as with a garment; the waters stood above the mountains. (vs. 5-6)

Then comes the appearance of land from the water (like Genesis 1:9):

> At Your rebuke they [the waters] fled, At the sound of Your thunder they hurried away. The mountains rose; the valleys sank down To the place which You established for them. (vs. 7-8)

So the continents came up, causing the water to run off. Then comes the punch line in verse 9:

> You set a boundary that they may not pass over, So that they will not return to cover the earth.

So, since the context for verse 9 is creation, the plain sense reading says that God made it so water would never cover the earth again. That points to a local flood, because under the universal flood, the water did cover the earth.

Geology?

Although geologists have discovered evidence of floods, including mega floods, none of them align with any worldwide picture of a universal flood. However, that's not necessarily surprising.

---

[7] My thanks to my colleague, James Rochford for this list of problems, http://www.evidenceunseen.com/articles/science-and-scripture/the-genesis-flood-global-or-local/.

The whole flood episode in Genesis took about a year. Geological rock strata don't tell us what happened in a given year. These strata take millions of years to form. Even identifying a particular millennium is usually impossible. An event that only lasted a year might not leave much behind, or even if it did, flood evidence might only show up in some locations, not in others.[8]

Ossiferous Fissures

Geologists point to something called "Ossiferous Fissures" for evidence of extraordinary floods in the past.

The fissures are deep crevasses or caves with the bones of thousands of animals, not related to each other. They routinely have skeletons from diverse animals, occasionally including human bones or tools.

These fissures are often found far above sea level, and usually have no stream or river geology associated with them. That's important, because at key bends in ancient rivers or tar pits you would expect to see a lot of fossils. This is the case, for instance, at Dinosaur National Park.

But in ossiferous fissures, complete animal skeletons are often found, separated and scattered. In other words, many of the animals died before being swept into the fissures.

Many of the bones are cast in a calcium compound that indicates water. Some are near or at the tops of hills, suggesting mixed animals went up to avoid rising water. The most common explanation for these fissures is a massive flood, and even secular scientists agree with that, though, of course, not a world flood.

But before getting too excited, note that these fissures do not originate from the same dates, and, although geologists

---

[8] Some discontinuities in the fossil record skip up to a billion years. In every case and at every age, discontinuities are evident when examining fossils worldwide. "A billion years missing from geologic record: Where it may have gone," https://www.sciencedaily.com/releases/2020/05/200507130704.htm.

accept that the cause is mega-floods, those floods appear to happen at different times in different localities.

Frozen mastodons and mammoths

Northern Siberia and other polar lands above the Arctic Circle contain a number of frozen mastodons and even more mammoths. They are frozen, sometimes with flesh intact, and even undigested food in their stomachs. A couple had grass still in their mouths. Therefore, they didn't die from hunger.

They didn't come from the regions where they were found, and neither does the food they were eating. It's easy to imagine that they were swept into the arctic by a flood maybe combined with rapid ocean currents, and that's what scientists believe happened.

Most frozen mammoths are dated 20,000 to 40,000 years ago. But, most importantly for viewing them as evidence of a world flood is that they are not from the same time period. Since the 1700's, scientists have found many examples, spread out over most of the twenty thousand years of their existence. That means they don't really point to a year-long flood.

You could completely discount the dating, but that's not warranted when dating organic tissue. Dating such tissues is much more reliable than dating simple minerals or even fossils that depend on the geological context.

Hyperbole?

Hyperbole (pronounced hi-_per_-bowl-ee) is a figure of speech especially common in the Bible, whose authors weren't encumbered with our western fixation on accuracy and precision. With hyperbole, the author deliberately exaggerates for effect, like saying, "Nobody believes that anymore." It really means most people don't believe that anymore. The exaggeration is given for emphasis.

Canadian scholar, Arthur Coustance, believes hyperbole is evident in Genesis 6-8. He gives a number of examples showing how the Bible uses this figure of speech more frequently than we do today. I've paraphrased some here:

1 Samuel 30:16 says the Amalekites were "being spread abroad upon all the earth" but really no more than the land of the Philistines (1 Samuel 29:11).

In Jeremiah 34:1, "Nebuchadnezzar king of Babylon and all his army, with all the kingdoms of the earth..." means those of "his dominion."

When Ahab sent his servant to find Elijah, he said, "As the Lord your God lives, there is no nation or kingdom where my lord has not sent to seek you" (1 Kings 18:10). He is really talking about the area around Israel.

2 Chronicles 36:23 says Cyrus' empire encompassed "all the kingdoms of the earth." Obviously, the kingdoms in the Far East, like China or Japan, were not included.

The New Testament is also full of hyperbole. The apostle James, in Jerusalem, points out that "Moses... has in every city those who preach Christ" (Acts 15:21). If he was worried about being precise, he would have said "most cities" or similar.

Paul claims in Colossians 1:23 that the Word of Life had actually been "preached to every creature under heaven," a clear case of hyperbole.

Luke 2:1 refers to a decree which went out to tax "the whole world," undoubtedly referring only to the Roman Empire.

In Acts 19:10 we are told that "all who dwell in Asia" had heard the gospel, really meaning most who dwell in Asia or maybe even many who dwell there.

It's not unreasonable to speak in this way. It's similar to saying: "I'm so hungry I could eat a horse"—a term we use without insisting on its literal meaning.[9]

So is it possible that Moses is using hyperbole here when referring to the flood? Local flood readers think he is.

Whether the flood was local or universal, it was definitely a supernatural event, unique in human history. The plausibility of the flood narrative depends on whether we spell God with a big "G" or a little "g." The God who spoke the universe into existence could definitely do a flood.

The ark

> Make for yourself an ark of gopher wood; you shall make the ark with rooms, and shall cover it inside and out with pitch.
>
> This is how you shall make it: the length of the ark three hundred cubits, its breadth fifty cubits, and its height thirty cubits.
>
> You shall make a window for the ark, and finish it to a cubit from the top; and set the door of the ark in the side of it; you shall make it with lower, second, and third decks. (Genesis 6:14-16)

This narrative is describing a four hundred and fifty foot-long oceangoing barge. No means of propulsion or steering is mentioned. It is designed to do what it did—drift and wait. That means the construction could be much lighter and less hydrodynamic than a normal ship.

An ark is a box, and that's probably what it looked like, not the swept bows you see in Sunday school pictures. A simple rectangular shape would also mean maximum useable square footage.

Square footage is not the only thing. Cubic footage would be immense, considering the almost twenty feet between

---

9 Arthur Coustance, *The Flood: Local or Global?*, (Grand Rapids: Zondervan; First Edition, 1979) 2nd Online Edition 2001 Chapter 1.

decks. Remember, not all animals are as big as a giraffe or
an elephant. Noah could have stacked cages, resulting in
room for many more species.

The animals?

> And of every living thing of all flesh, you shall bring
> two of every kind into the ark, to keep them alive
> with you; they shall be male and female. Of the birds
> after their kind, and of the animals after their kind,
> of every creeping thing of the ground after its kind,
> two of every kind will come to you to keep them alive.
> (Genesis 6:19-20)

A good question for local flood interpreters is, why did God
have Noah bring the animals into the ark? Why would this
be necessary if the flood was local? They answer that these
would have been the relatively few species from the area
affected—Mesopotamia.

In fact, that makes it way more plausible that the ark could
fit enough species. How different the view under a universal
flood—to put two or even seven pairs of every species on
earth—and enough food for them all to eat for a year. That's
clearly impossible. And impossibility is one of the key
reasons for seeing figures of speech.

If the species were only those in the area of the Fertile
Crescent, the effort would be less to avoid extinction and
more to quickly repopulate the area.

Scientists have recently estimated that there are
approximately 8.7 million species on Earth and 1-2 million
of those are animals. So hyperbole is again evident here.

God also distinguished between clean and unclean animals.
"You shall take with you of every clean animal by sevens, a
male and his female; and of the animals that are not clean
two, a male and his female" (7:2). The most plausible
reason for the difference is that clean animals could also
serve the need for food.

All humans?

Another problem for the local view is that the text says all humans were destroyed except for Noah's family. To this, local flood readers answer in two ways.

First, under some scenarios, humans had not spread out very far yet, so a local flood would have been enough to lay waste to the whole race. Under this view, the flood would have happened near the time of creation.[10]

Others argue that the "all flesh" or "all mankind" mentioned here is again relative to the area in view—basically the Fertile Crescent. These were the people God was dealing with in connection with his future plan. The whole of Genesis seems to deal with this area, which includes the land of Israel.

Could there have been other populations in remote continents or islands? Anthropological and archeological finds suggest populations were present in most parts of the world far back into the Stone Age. It's not clear what the theological implications of this would be, but the text favors the idea that the flood only spared Noah's family: "The Lord said, 'I will blot out man whom I have created from the face of the land'" (Genesis 6:7). Could this mean only people in this area or "land?"

Water

Local flood theorists press the point that to cover the tallest mountains would require several times the water on earth. Where did all this water come from and where did it go?

Of course, the one who created the universe could have called water into existence and out of existence afterward. But the picture is rather far-fetched. Why go through a

---

[10] This is quite possible if you go by the minimum time frame for the genealogies in Genesis 5 discussed earlier. The minimum reading probably entails either a young earth creation (which I believe should be discarded) or a gap type creation. In a word, it seems like the gap theory is tied to any possibility of a local flood. Of course, any creation theory is compatible with a universal flood.

natural event, like a flood, instead of simply blowing all humans away?

This problem may have recently evaporated because of research indicating that Earth has way more water than we ever guessed. The transition zone between earth's inner and outer mantle, a region about 410 to 660 kilometers from the surface, has been found to contain vast quantities of water.

Andrew Williams (quoting Steve Jacobsen of Northwestern University) says, "If there is just 1 to 2 percent H_2O by weight in the transition zone, that would be equivalent to 2 to 3 times the amount of water in all of our oceans,"[11] Woo agrees.

> Considering that the transition zone is a roughly 250-kilometer-thick shell that accounts for about 7 percent of Earth's mass (by comparison, the crust is only 1 percent), it could contain several times the water of Earth's oceans.[12]

Notice that the biblical text is clear that the water came down, but *also up*.

> In the six hundredth year of Noah's life, in the second month, on the seventeenth day of the month, on the same day *all the fountains of the great deep burst open*, and the floodgates of the sky were opened. (Genesis 6:11, emphasis added)

So the "fountains of the deep" could refer to accessing this massive store of water.

While it's not clear what kind of seismic event would make possible the release of water from the transition zone, I

---

11 Andrew Williams, "Scientists Detect Evidence of 'Oceans worth' of Water in Earth's Mantle," *Astrobiology Magazine*, Aug 21, 2014. See also Andy Coghlan, "There's as much water in Earth's mantle as in all the oceans," *NewScientist*, June 7 2017.

12 Marcus Woo, "The Hunt for Earth's Deep Hidden Oceans," *Quanta Magazine*, July 11, 2018.

think it's significant that so much water is right here already on our planet.

Flood stories?

Universal flood interpreters argue that the widespread flood stories in cultures with no connection to each other strengthen the universal view. These stories not only say that a flood occurred, they also have many of the same details, including a single family surviving. Sometimes they built an ark, or a large canoe. In other cases, they went to the top of the tallest mountain.

The Babylonians, Sumerians, and Assyrians all were in a position to borrow from each other, as was the Old Testament. In fact, liberal scholars claim Genesis is borrowed from the Babylonians' *Gilgamesh Epic*.[13]

But most of the stories come from cultures that have no involvement with each other at any time in their histories. For instance, Hindu scriptures tell of Manu, who was warned of the flood and escaped in a large boat with his three sons and three daughters, just like Noah.

The Chinese tell of Fah-He, who escaped the flood with his three sons and three daughters in a big canoe. Hawaiians tell of Nu-U. Mesoamericans have a number of accounts, as do European peoples, and throughout Asia.

In all, over 270 flood myths have been found, and the number increases as we study the lore of more tribal peoples.[14]

---

[13] The theology and content are utterly different. For instance, the highest god Enlil decides to destroy the world with a flood because humans have become too noisy. The similarities are in the most trivial aspects of vocabulary, which are shared as in much of ancient near eastern language groups. Thus argues Alexander Heidel, *The Gilgamesh Epic and Old Testament Parallels*, (Chicago: University of Chicago Press, 1963) where you can read *Gilgamesh* in translation for yourself and compare.

[14] To give an idea how much testimony this is, consider Will Durant, a British scholar, who was so skeptical of anything biblical that he openly doubted that Jesus even existed! Yet he says of the lost civilization of Atlantis, "We cannot entirely ignore the legends...." The Atlantis myth is based on a total of three accounts, but scholars, including Durant, believe one is based directly on another,

Is it possible that these stories represent a shared memory of the time when God wiped out most of humanity? Before jumping too hard on that conclusion, consider that all of these accounts (except for Genesis) are mythopoeic, not historical. The characters in these stories routinely turn into giant animals or insects and attack each other—anything goes in these dreamlike stories.

Also, the other myths are amoral. Unlike the biblical story, which is highly moral, the other flood myths lack the concept of objective morality. They portray capricious and strange gods doing crazy things without any reference to moral good or evil.

You also have to wonder, if peoples in Hawaii, South America, Scandinavia, and Polynesia all remember the flood, how much time passed after the flood for all these areas to be populated, beginning with one family? And how long do cultures remember an event like this?

An alternative explanation would be that Satan is the great counterfeiter who regularly bastardizes elements in the biblical account, adding them to other religious systems. These are similar in some ways, but fatally different at the central point.

For example, consider how animal sacrifice is found widely in unrelated religions, but the reason is different—usually to feed hungry gods! That's nothing like Old Testament sacrifice which is for atonement or thanksgiving. Atoning for the people's moral wrongdoing is almost completely absent from animal sacrifice lore in other religions.[15] So the proliferation of flood accounts could be viewed as discrediting the biblical account.

---

so there are really only two. *The Story of Civilization, Volume I, Our Oriental Heritage*, (NY: MJF Books, 1993).

[15] A fascinating read on parallel themes in world religions is Mircea Eliade, *Patterns in Comparative Religion*, (University of Nebraska Press, Bison Books; Reprint edition, 1996).

Finally, widespread flood stories could also fit a local flood, because people would have spread out after the time of Noah, bringing their memories with them.

Harsh?

This whole story is jarring, not just because it involves amazing supernatural power, but because it results in the horrific destruction of nearly everyone on earth.

When thinking about this mass judgment, consider the following:

- First, we need to try to view this event from the view of an eternal God who sees time differently than we do. God already knew that humans would all die as a result of the fall, and that happens one hundred percent of the time. If he then decides to shorten or lengthen someone's life within that envelope, that's not an ultimate tragedy.

- Physical death is not the worst thing that can happen to someone. Ending up eternally separated from God is a lot worse.

- Events like the destruction of Sodom and Gomorrah raise the same question, and it's the key question in this whole area: Does God have the right to judge humans? Put differently, is God right or wrong when he judges? As believers, we can only answer that God has that right and that his judgments are correct. As Abraham suggested, "Shall not the Judge of all the earth deal justly?" (Genesis 18:25).

- Babies and children were taken to heaven, something that probably wouldn't have happened if they grew up.[16]

---

[16] Scripture teaches that children too young to grasp their need for grace are taken to heaven. See 2 Samuel 12:15–23, where David says he will see his dead infant son later in the afterlife. Also, Jesus said his father loves children in Matthew 19:13–15 and parallels.

- This is not the last time God will destroy much of the human race. Jesus will slay the wicked with the sword of his mouth when he returns (Revelation 19:21).

So, like it or not, God is a judging God. Considering what we deserve, it's less remarkable that God might strike down humans, than that he made it possible for them to be rescued through Jesus.

The big picture

People have asked me, "So what do you tell people when they ask whether the flood was local or universal?" I answer that I tell them the truth—I don't know. I see a lot of tensions for either view. But the text can be read in more than one way. I believe all humans died in the flood, but that could be true for either a local or universal view.

26 The Genesis Flood: Theology

Genesis 6-8

Preparation

God instructed Noah:

> Make for yourself an ark of gopher wood; you shall make the ark with rooms, and shall cover it inside and out with pitch. This is how you shall make it: the length of the ark three hundred cubits, its breadth fifty cubits, and its height thirty cubits. You shall make a window for the ark, and finish it to a cubit from the top; and set the door of the ark in the side of it; you shall make it with lower, second, and third decks. (Genesis 6:14-16)

Three hundred cubits is four hundred and fifty feet or more. With the width of about fifty feet, and three levels, the square footage was about 80,000 square feet. But the decks were almost twenty feet apart vertically, so the cubic feet would be a whopping 3.9 million!

Although this would have been far larger than any ship of its time, remember it didn't really sail. I just sat and drifted.

Noah's faith

The more we imagine Noah and his family constructing the ark, the more we are stunned by his radical faith. Noah didn't live on the coast. He is probably living many miles from the nearest navigable body of water. How bizarre his behavior must have looked to his neighbors!

The time it took to build this massive barge was over a hundred years. During all of that time, we have no indication that God was talking to Noah or his family. I can imagine on the 108th year, looking back. "I'm sure I had that conversation with you God.... right?" Even one month before the flood, there was no trend to look at, no external sign that the flood was drawing near; nothing but God's word, spoken a long time ago.

Hebrews 11:7 declares,

> By faith Noah, being warned by God about things not yet seen, in reverence prepared an ark for the salvation of his household, by which he condemned the world, and became an heir of the righteousness which is according to faith.

The statement that "he condemned the world" is simply referring to his cooperation with God's decision to judge the world, and his completion of the ark opened the door for the flood. The important point here is that he did what he did "by faith."

Although we have not been called on for anything at the same level Noah was, we, too, need to live by faith. Was Noah countercultural in his way of life? Absolutely! He was so countercultural they no doubt thought he was completely insane.

But was he insane? Not at all. His non-believing neighbors couldn't understand his family's extreme devotion to a project that seemed so absurd. But we know better.

We are also called to be countercultural. Our culture insists on a relative view of truth, never criticizing anyone's moral standards or beliefs, and giving your all to your career and financial success. We can't expect them to easily understand why we think the things of God are so important.

Too often, Christians have lost their way and end up conforming to their neighbors. They become too busy for the things of God. They become unwilling to invest enough time and effort to build real community in the church. Not many are willing to withstand the stinging criticism we can expect if we follow the path of Noah.

As we read the description of the ark, we notice the massive door, running down the side and extending upward three floors. Made out of timbers, it must have weighed thousands of pounds. During construction, it lay out like a big gang plank. But God gave no provision for closing the door. Was there a system of pulleys? How did they seal the perimeter of the door to make it water tight?

The answer comes in Chapter 7:16 where we read that they entered the ark, "and God closed it behind them." That answers a lot of questions—not only why God provided no closing plan for the door. The more important question was, "Who gets to be rescued in the ark?"

The offer to enter the ark was theoretically open to all. In 2 Peter 2:5 we learn that Noah was a "preacher of righteousness." He must have stopped work while building and preached to his godless neighbors. Nobody listened to him, but he continued to tell them anyway.

When the door to the ark closed, it was a solemn, grave occasion, because it was a one-way event. The door would not be opened again for late comers. How could Noah ever decide to close it, knowing that everyone he knew would be destroyed if he did? He couldn't. Closing the ark wasn't for him to decide. God closed the door.

God closes the door still today. Whether at our death or at his coming, the freedom to choose is limited. Once we reach that limit, it's too late.

When the door closed, rain began to fall and sea water began rolling up from the south. Now things looked completely different. Noah no longer looked like a fool or a crazy person. What a sickening realization people must have experienced as the water deepened—to look over at the ark and realize Noah had been right the whole time!

We can always change our mind... but only up to a point. Human choice is free, but not infinite. At some point in time, our decision is final.

We all will decide. If we do nothing, that's a decision in itself. Jesus said in Matthew 12:30, "He who is not with Me is against Me; and he who does not gather with Me scatters."

The journey ended

> But God remembered Noah and all the beasts and all the cattle that were with him in the ark; and God caused a wind to pass over the earth, and the water subsided. Also the fountains of the deep and the floodgates of the sky were closed, and the rain from the sky was restrained; and the water receded steadily from the earth, and at the end of one hundred and fifty days the water decreased. (Genesis 8:1-3)

Notice that, again, it wasn't enough to stop the rain. God also needed to close "the fountains of the deep." As suggested earlier, this could refer to some opening that permitted access to the vast stores of water in the earth's mantle. It could also refer to massive aquifers that contain millions of cubic kilometers of water, much nearer the earth's surface.

It could also refer to melt water from the last ice age that we know raised the sea level worldwide by hundreds of feet. But the problem is that the melting event wouldn't fit within a year-long flood.

> In the seventh month, on the seventeenth day of the month, the ark rested upon the mountains of Ararat. (8:4)

This is not necessarily saying that the ark grounded on the summit of today's 17,000 foot Mt. Ararat in Turkey. The term is in the plural, suggesting a range of hills or mountains. Today's Mt. Ararat only got its name long after Noah's flood. Wikipedia correctly explains, "The mountain has been called by the name Ararat since the Middle Ages

[AD.], as it began to be identified with 'mountains of Ararat' described in the Bible as the resting place of Noah's Ark.[1]

This is significant in the local/universal flood debate. Any flood capable of depositing the ark on the summit of modern Ararat would definitely inundate the whole world. But if the ark came to rest on one of the smaller hills in Armenia, a local flood remains possible.

> The waters continued to recede until the tenth month, and on the first day of the tenth month the tops of the mountains became visible. (v. 8:5)

The chronology in this chapter isn't easy to follow, but commentators have worked it out without contradiction. Here, the mountain tops must be distant, because the ark continues to float. The fact that he sees distant mountains confirms the view that the ark did not land on the summit of Ararat. If that were the case, there would be no other mountains to see, because Ararat is by far the tallest mountain within sight in that part of the world.

> After forty days Noah opened the window he had made in the ark and sent out a raven, and it kept flying back and forth until the water had dried up from the earth. (vs. 6-7)

Forty more days? That's the way most take it. It isn't saying this was the first time he opened the window. It sounds like Noah hadn't counted on the raven's soaring ability. Next time he let out a dove.

> Then he sent out a dove to see if the water had receded from the surface of the ground. But the dove could find no place to set its feet because there was water over all the surface of the earth [or land]; so it returned to Noah in the ark. He reached out his hand and took the dove and brought it back to himself in the ark. He waited seven more days and

---

[1] https://en.wikipedia.org/wiki/Mount_Ararat. They add, "the word [*uratu*] referred to the wider region at the time and not specifically to Mt. Ararat."

> again sent out the dove from the ark. When the dove returned to him in the evening, there in its beak was a freshly plucked olive leaf! Then Noah knew that the water had receded from the earth [or land]. He waited seven more days and sent the dove out again, but this time it did not return to him. (vs. 8-12)

Again, Noah doesn't know what conditions are, or how long it will take for land in his area to reappear. He has to experiment in order to find out. So the story is told from Noah's perspective, not from that of an omniscient narrator, like much of the narrative in the Old Testament.

Although I argued earlier that these antediluvian accounts were not handed down in writing or verbally, I have to admit that this account includes the kind of minute detail that you would expect from a firsthand account.

Or maybe God showed Moses a movie-like vision and he recounted in words? We don't know. But in this section, the reader discovers what is happening as Noah discovers it, not by divine statement.

This is significant because in a local flood, a spectator like Noah might see endless water even though land is uncovered elsewhere (the curvature of the earth severely limits how far one can see across the ocean or even a large lake).

If this scenario is true, we have *perspectival language* (language from the perspective of the speaker) in addition to hyperbole. With perspectival language, the speaker may say things that aren't true everywhere, but they are true from his perspective. Just because Noah couldn't see land, doesn't necessarily mean it wasn't showing in other areas.

Typology

The ark was a vessel people could enter in order to be saved from coming judgment. In that sense, it resembles Jesus. We are baptized into Jesus in spiritual baptism, according to 1 Corinthians 12:13, "For by one Spirit we were all baptized into one body."

That's what Peter is talking about when he says,

> The patience of God kept waiting in the days of Noah, during the construction of the ark, in which a few, that is, eight persons, were brought safely through the water. Corresponding to that, baptism now saves you—not the removal of dirt from the flesh, but an appeal to God for a good conscience—through the resurrection of Jesus Christ. (1 Peter 3:20-21)

Some people think Peter is teaching baptismal regeneration—that salvation is based on water baptism—when he says "baptism now saves you." But that's wrong. Too many readers are eager to understand the word "baptism" to mean water baptism, although it often refers to something else.[2]

In this case, people were not baptized (a word that means "put into") into water. Rather it was the non-believers who were baptized into water. The believers were baptized into the ark—a type, or symbol, of Jesus. This baptism is spiritual baptism, and it really does save.

By identifying believers with Jesus through spiritual baptism, God can look at us as he looks at his Son. 2 Corinthians 5:21 uses the term "in him" to explain how we become acceptable to God: "He made him who knew no sin to be sin on our behalf, so that we might become the righteousness of God in Him."

So the salvation of Noah's family in the ark becomes a picture that holds true throughout the Bible—God reaching out to win and rescue his people from the judgment to come.

---

[2] Jesus said "But I have a baptism to undergo, and how distressed I am until it is accomplished!" (Luke 12:50). He was referring to his suffering and death. In Matthew 3:11, John the Baptist said, "As for me, I baptize you with water for repentance, but He who is coming after me ...will baptize you with the Holy Spirit and fire." So baptism can refer to being put into other things besides water.

The big picture

God expressed great sorrow when he announced the coming judgment on humanity. Judgment should be a sad event for us as well. Avoiding judgment ourselves and showing others how they can avoid it must rank as one of the most important things we can do.

How blessed we are that God has provided us an ark in Jesus. We, our families, and our friends can have eternal security in him.

27 The Noahic Covenant
Genesis 9:1-17

God announces the covenant

Right before the flood, God made a promise:

> Behold, I, even I am bringing the flood of water upon
> the earth…. But I will establish my covenant with
> you; and you shall enter the ark—you and your sons
> and your wife, and your sons' wives with you.
> (Genesis 6:17-18)

Here we have the first mention of a "covenant" between God
and people in the Bible.

A covenant is a pledge or agreement much like contracts
today. The covenant could be between people or
governments. Some covenants were co-equal; others were
between an overlord and a vassal state. A vassal state is
any state that has an obligation to a superior state or
empire.

Covenants were often used when forming alliances, and
usually involved an oath between the parties. They often
erected a stone to commemorate the agreement, and
usually called on deities to witness the oaths.[1]

In the Bible, a covenant is a side-deal God makes with
people of faith. It usually doesn't apply to everyone. They
are agreements that allow closeness between God and
people.

---

[1] These instances of covenant formation among people and nations help explain
what covenants were. Genesis 15:18; 31:44–47; 31:54–55; Joshua 9; 1 Sam 18:3;
20:8; 23:18; 2 Sam 21; 1 Kings 9:16; Amos 1:9. In Israel's monarchy the covenant
relationship between the people and the king provided a kind of limited
constitutional monarchy which was unique in the world in that early age (2 Sam
3:21; 5:3; 1 Chronicles 11:3). E. B. Smick in R. Laird Harris et al., TWOT, 129.

Biblical covenants are all proposed by God in light of the fallenness of the world. So they are the result of God's initiating love. Noah never spent a minute wondering what he should do about a coming flood. He had no idea. It was God who knew it was coming and who took steps to make sure the believers in Noah's family were rescued and given a new covenant afterward.

It's no different than Jesus' coming and death. Nobody was calling out to God pleading for him to send an atoning messiah. It was all his idea and his initiative. All we can do is respond. This initiating element is a crucial part of true, biblical love.

So the mention of covenant here is a positive ray of light. God shows himself ready to meet with people, to promise a relationship with them, and to outline the details of behavior which will make this promised relationship warm and wholesome.

Once this idea of covenant was introduced in scripture, the theme persists right through to the new covenant, sealed in the blood of Christ.[2]

In Genesis 8:21-22 we read,

> And the Lord said to his soul, "I will never again curse the ground on account of man, for the intent of man's heart is evil from his youth; and I will never again destroy every living thing, as I have done.
>
> While the earth remains, seedtime and harvest, and cold and heat, and summer and winter, and day and night shall not cease."

It's a comforting passage, and a promise he has kept. How steady and reliable our seasonal rotation and our steady sun are! Seasons slowly but steadily come turning through and our food grows. Natural disasters happen, but nothing on this scale.

---

[2]D. Stuart Briscoe and Lloyd J. Ogilvie, vol. 1, *The Preacher's Commentary Series, Volume 1: Genesis*, (Nashville, TN: Thomas Nelson Inc, 1987) 82.

God speaks to himself here first, as a triune God, and then goes and repeats it to the people.

Noah was introduced to a new sense of security. Was this pattern of the world becoming polluted, and God destroying it, going to keep happening over and over? No.

God's commitment was not based on man's worthiness. His statement was made at the same time he reiterated the sad fact of man's unrelenting evil, and his disapproval, "...for the intent of man's heart is evil from his youth."

We see several similarities with the original covenant when humans were created, but key differences added because of the entrance of sin.

Being fruitful

> Then God blessed Noah and his sons and told them, "Be fruitful and multiply. Fill the earth. (v. 1)

This commission echoes Genesis 1. Now that the world is devoid of humans beyond this family, the call makes sense. Conditions have changed in our day, and this commission to fill the earth has already been completed, so it doesn't apply any longer.

Fear of humans

> All the animals of the earth, all the birds of the sky, all the small animals that scurry along the ground, and all the fish in the sea will look on you with fear and dread. I have placed them in your power. (Genesis 9:2)

Man was still in charge of the animal kingdom and the agent of the divine rule, but a new note had crept in. Under Adam's rule there was no suggestion of tension between man and the animal kingdom. But for Noah there would be a difference— *"And the fear of you and the dread of you will be on every beast."*

Eating animals

> I have given them to you for food, just as I have given
> you grain and vegetables. But you must never eat
> any meat that still has the lifeblood in it. (Genesis
> 9:3-4)

We see repetition between this covenant and God's original
commission of humans in Chapter 1. This passage is not
teaching that people never ate meat before this decree.
That's ridiculous. People had been herding and hunting
animals for thousands of years. Rather, this is a new
beginning with much repetition from earlier covenants.

Murder

> And I will require the blood of anyone who takes
> another person's life. If a wild animal kills a person,
> it must die. And anyone who murders a fellow
> human must die. If anyone takes a human life, that
> person's life will also be taken by human hands. For
> God made human beings in his own image. (Genesis
> 9:5-6)

The main stress here is the importance of a human being,
created in the image of God.

Humans, made in God's image, had shown themselves
capable of taking others' lives, and this was totally
unacceptable to God. Humans had to be protected from
themselves.

Capital punishment

While these verses and the Mosaic covenant seem to argue
in favor of capital punishment, a case can still be made that
under modern conditions, capital punishment has become
unjust.

In our society people sit on death row for decades before
their execution—a practice never envisioned in the Bible.
Arguably, our system is much crueler than theirs.

Also, unlike ancient village culture, where people knew each other, modernity has created a situation where most of us have no idea who our neighbors are. A perpetrator is usually unknown to the community. That could lead to more mistakes and less deterrence.

Modern perpetrators are executed in secrecy before a handful of people, and that further decreases any deterrent for society as a whole. In ancient times, people would have watched executions or even participated in them (in the case of stoning).

Finally, the Innocence Project, and other groups have proven that innocent people are being executed in the U.S. The death penalty also falls on African Americans multiple times more frequently than on white criminals. The poor are many times more likely than the wealthy to be executed.

These factors cause me to believe that, under modern conditions, the death penalty is no longer just.

If an animal killed a man, killing the animal could hardly be regarded as retribution but rather a statement, required to emphasize the importance of image-bearers. Here is why racism or other forms of prejudice are wrong. Humans get their high value because they are created in God's image.

Eating the blood with the flesh was also regarded as unacceptable because it later turns out that blood is reserved for atonement. We have no record of God decreeing this until Leviticus 17:10-11, but these early believers seem to know about animal sacrifice, so he probably told them at some point and it wasn't recorded.

Confirmation

> Then God told Noah and his sons, "I hereby confirm my covenant with you and your descendants, and with all the animals that were on the boat with you— the birds, the livestock, and all the wild animals— every living creature on earth. Yes, I am confirming

my covenant with you. Never again will floodwaters kill all living creatures; never again will a flood destroy the earth [or land." (Genesis 9:8-11)

The rainbow

Then God said, "I am giving you a sign of my covenant with you and with all living creatures, for all generations to come. I have placed my rainbow in the clouds. It is the sign of my covenant with you and with all the earth.... Then God said to Noah, "Yes, this rainbow is the sign of the covenant I am confirming with all the creatures on earth." (vs. 12-17)

The extent of the covenant is seen in the use of "*everlasting*" and "*all flesh.*" This was not a covenant for some people but not others (like most covenants). It was for everyone, except that the blood part has been fulfilled in Jesus' death.

Most covenants have some symbol or reminder assigned by God. The Abrahamic covenant had circumcision. The Mosaic covenant had Passover. The New Covenant has the Last Supper. Here, it's the rainbow.

The big picture

The flood was a new beginning. The depravity of humans was becoming so intense and universal that nothing less than a complete judgment could save the situation.

God was reluctant to judge, like always. But after the flood, he made the promise that he would never again flood the earth. The beautiful reminder of that promise was the rainbow. The passage never claims that this was the first rainbow or that this is how rainbows came to be. Nothing is said to that effect. God simply took a phenomenon we see periodically and used it as a reminder of his promise.

28 Noah and His Sons

Genesis 9:18-29

Noah's story isn't over. As his family disembarked from the ark, our attention is drawn to his sons:

> Now the sons of Noah who came out of the ark were Shem and Ham and Japheth; and Ham was the father of Canaan. These three were the sons of Noah, and from these the whole earth was populated. (Genesis 9:18-19)

Notice that, although all three had sons, only Ham's son, Canaan is mentioned. This comes up later. In the next two chapters, Moses will explain how these descendants migrated. But before that, he felt the need to tell one more story about Noah.

Noah's disgrace

> Then Noah began farming and planted a vineyard. He drank of the wine and became drunk, and uncovered himself inside his tent. Ham, the father of Canaan, saw the nakedness of his father, and told his two brothers outside. But Shem and Japheth took a garment and laid it upon both their shoulders and walked backward and covered the nakedness of their father; and their faces were turned away, so that they did not see their father's nakedness. (Genesis 9:20-23)

What Noah did was shameful. This is truly pathetic. He must have been really drunk—pass out drunk! Why did God include this account at the end of Noah's story? Was it because of the significance of the cursing of Ham (see below)? Or was it a warning that even awesome followers of God can lose it and fall into shameful sin, especially when they're older and more complacent? We see far too many older men and women of God finish poorly, leaving a sad footnote on their lives.

The sons' reactions

Ham was probably inadvertently confronted with Noah's shame. It must have been shocking. But he could think of nothing better to do than run to his brothers, "Check this out!" Ham would be judged for this disrespectful response. Even though Noah was in sin, he was still Ham's father.[1]

Japheth and Shem discreetly averted their eyes, and respectfully covered the old man's nakedness. The account implies that this was the right thing to do.

Noah's curse and blessing

> When Noah awoke from his wine, he knew what his youngest son had done to him. So he said, cursed be Canaan; a servant of servants he shall be to his brothers." He also said, "Blessed be the Lord, the God of Shem; And let Canaan be his servant. "May God enlarge Japheth, and let him dwell in the tents of Shem; and let Canaan be his servant." (Genesis 9:24-27)

So Noah curses Canaan, Ham's son, instead of Ham himself. Canaan became the father of the Canaanite peoples who were warlike, blood thirsty, and perpetuated religions that were erotic and savage, including human sacrifice of children. They would be a thorn in Israel's side for centuries to come. This curse anticipates that future history, and is therefore prophetic.

---

[1] A much later interpretation, found in some rabbinic and church fathers' commentaries was that Ham sexually assaulted his dad while he was passed out. The reasons for this view are 1) the curse seems too strong for a trivial sin and 2) the text says Noah "knew what his youngest son had done to him." So, it is argued, Ham actually did something really bad. But the text doesn't call for such an improbable thing between two very old men. In ancient culture, simply shaming a parent was considered plenty serious. Besides, Noah was speaking a prophetic word that might not have been solely related to the sin of Ham.

Shem is the father of the "Shemites" or Semites, which includes the Jews. Noah mentions "Yahweh, the God of Shem." So it would be Shem's descendents who would take the lead in preserving the knowledge of God on earth.

Japheth gets blessed in the sense of fertility and expansion—major concerns at this time of repopulation.

It's important to see that this proclamation was prediction, not causality. As someone who was close to God, Noah here, as earlier, had the privilege of hearing prediction of the future.

The big picture

Noah's faithfulness resulted in the survival of the human race. As they spread out to create farms, the people immediately after Noah continued to live to relatively great ages. Fertility was probably quite high.

Unfortunately, people learned little from the judgment of the flood. As they fanned out, we quickly see them drift back into animistic religion, and the memory of the true God nearly disappeared.

29 The Table of Nations

Genesis 10

What is it?

Genesis 10 contains a description of what happened to Noah's children and the peoples who came from them. The list has traditionally been called the "Table of Nations."

It's a unique piece of literature with no parallel in any ancient literature of its time. Other genealogies are only concerned with their own lineage. As you study the pathways, you quickly realize that Moses had no way to know this on his own, let's say, from stories passed down or travels he, or someone he knew took.

Some of it could have come from his education in Egypt, but I think it's doubtful, because such knowledge would have been flawed and not suitable to add to an inspired and infallible text. This table is far too sweeping and broad for that. It had to be revealed directly from God.

The liberal view is exemplified by Gordon Wenham:

> The majority of scholars prefer a first-millennium date for the composition of this chapter, because some of the peoples listed here are not mentioned in extra biblical texts until then.[1]

In other words, the Bible is always false until and unless we can verify it from secular sources. This method invariably discredits the Bible. Instead, the later references to these peoples shows that the Bible is the most ancient reference to them—a mark of authenticity.

---

[1] Gordon J. Wenham, *Word Biblical Commentary* Vol. 1, Genesis 1-15, (Dallas: Word, Inc., 2002) 213.

Ancient Jewish historian Josephus wrote a fascinating account of who each of these sons were and who they correspond to in his day (1st century AD).[2] He refers to a number of other historians of his day and earlier who he says agree with his coverage, including several no longer available today.

The coverage begins in the eastern fertile crescent and follows movements of early humans to the North, West, and South. The Table doesn't cover eastward movements, probably because Genesis is ultimately a book about the children of Israel. Most of these peoples are peoples Israel had to deal with. Those who went east pass out of this story.

The Table never claims to be exhaustive in coverage. It covers the peoples of interest to the Genesis account. The fact that God caused this chapter to be included speaks to the global perspective of God's program for mankind, later articulated to Abraham—"in you all the families of the earth will be blessed" (Genesis 12:3).

An interesting refrain appears three times:

> From these the coastlands of the nations were separated into their lands, every one according to his language, according to their families, into their nations. (Genesis 10:5 see also v. 20, 31)

This refrain is admitting that much more could be said. They are like an ellipsis marking places where the further developments pass out of interest for the current narrative.

Even several of the later nations that came into close contact with Israel, such as Moab, Ammon, Edom, and Amalek, find no mention here, although we can safely say most of them are from the line of Ham (Canaan) and Edom is from the line of Shem as covered later in the text.

---

[2] Flavius Josephus, *Antiquities of the Jews*, Book 1, Chapter 6, "After what manner the posterity of Noah sent out Colonies, and inhabited the whole earth."

Ross argues that, "the concern of the writer is to fit the Table to the message of the book: the fulfillment of God's promise to bless Israel as a nation in that land, and to bless those nations that bless her, and curse those who are antagonistic to her.[3]

This Table is another example of the literary pattern in Genesis. It deals with the broad sweep of history first, and only after that stops to consider the last figure. In this case, that brings us first to Nimrod, then Abraham.[4]

Earlier, it was the six days of creation followed by the detailed story of the sixth day. Then the descendants of Cain before those of Seth (chapters 4–5). Later, Esau (Chapter 36) before Jacob (Chapters 37–50).

The pattern is significant because it shows that Genesis is a unified, coherent story, and that the first chapters are laid out no differently than the later ones. Higher critics and neo-evangelicals divide chapters 1-11 from what follows mainly out of unbelief, not out of sound literary analysis.

Once this table shows the nations' kinship with the chosen people, they are dismissed from the Scripture record, and attention shifts to the Semitic line.

Japheth

> The sons of Japheth were Gomer and Magog and Madai and Javan and Tubal and Meshech and Tiras. (v. 2)

The movement of peoples in this account matches roughly similar directional maps developed in modern times based on language development and mitochondrial DNA studies. Anthropologists' migratory maps showing how they believe

---

[3] Allen P. Ross, "The Table of Nations in Genesis 10—Its Content" *Bibliotheca Sacra*, 138 (1980) 30.

[4] Chapter 11 traces Shem's descendants further through Eber, father of Peleg. It ends in Serug, Nahor, and Terah, Abraham's father. Eber is linguistically linked to "Hebrews."

the world was populated, beginning in Mesopotamia, match this table rather well.

Of course, anthropologists think that even earlier, humans migrated from Africa into Mesopotamia. That part isn't mentioned in the Bible. It could have happened before the six days of Genesis 1 for people accepting a gap theory of creation.[5] As far as this list goes, the migration is from the middle east *into* Africa.

Secular scholars also argue for a coastal migration to the east into India and China. That doesn't contradict anything in this account. However, the secular dating for all the migrations out of Mesopotamia are way back to 60 to 75 thousand years ago, far earlier than this account, in the view of most Bible scholars.

The Japeth tribal groups migrated from the eastern fertile crescent north into Anatolia and through the Caucasus into the Steppe of southern Russia. From there, they may have spread east into Asia (although that movement is not recounted here), and from Anatolia northwest into Europe through modern Turkey and Ukraine.

These people come up again in the book of Ezekiel, where they participate in an unprovoked attack on the regathered nation of Israel.[6]

> The sons of Gomer were Ashkenaz and Riphath and Togarmah. The sons of Javan were Elishah and Tarshish, Kittim and Dodanim. (vs. 3-4)

---

[5] It's important to remember that the African finds by the Leaky's are not necessarily human. Most are believed to be related to humans by secular Anthropologists. See earlier discussion on the possible role of hominids in Chapter 6.

[6] "Gog," "Magog," "Tubal," and "Meshek" all appear in Ezek 27:13; 32:26; 38:2-3; 39:1. Wenham adds, "Cuneiform texts locate Muški and Tabāl in central and eastern Anatolia. Herodotus (1.14) describes Midas as a Phrygian." "In the Greek sources they are called the Moschoi and Tibarenoi (Herodotus 3.94; 7.78)." and, "The Scythians came from southern Russia, driving the Cimmerians ahead of them... "Kittim" is usually identified with the island of Cyprus. Gordon Wenham, *Genesis*, 217. Ezekiel also says these peoples are mostly lie to the north of Israel (39:2).

These grandsons and the tribes coming from them lived mostly to the north and east of Canaan and spoke the Indo-European languages, according to Hughes. Gomer dwelt north of the Caspian Sea.[7] Tubal and Meshech settled around the southern shores of the Black Sea.

Tiras is believed to have lived west of the Black Sea in Thrace. Madai occupied the area south of the Caspian in what became Media. These are the "Medes" of the Medo-Persian empire centuries later.

Javan populated Ionia, the southern part of Greece. The sons of Javan spread around the northern Mediterranean as far west as Tarshish, or southern Spain.

All the maritime coastlands and island areas surrounding the Mediterranean are from the line of Japheth. He is the father of European Gentiles, according to this table.

Selectivity

> From these the coastlands of the nations were separated into their lands, every one according to his language, according to their families, into their nations. (v. 5)

This closing summary differs from the other two by emphasizing *"the islands of the Gentiles."* or literally, *"coastlands of the Gentiles."* It's an expression used in the Old Testament to refer to all the distant lands bordering the Mediterranean.

These closing markers also stress that there is much more to say, but the account is only covering chosen migrations. The others are not of interest because they don't have relevance to the plan God is describing.

Ham

The descendants of Ham later became the Canaanites, Africans, and some parts of the Fertile Crescent.

---

[7] Kent Hughes *Genesis,* 157.

> The sons of Ham were Cush and Mizraim and Put
> and Canaan. The sons of Cush were Seba and
> Havilah and Sabtah and Raamah and Sabteca; and
> the sons of Raamah were Sheba and Dedan. (vs. 6-7)

It looks like some of these peoples stayed in the Babylonian area, while some migrated across Arabia and in to Africa. Miozraim is the Hebrew word for the land of Egypt. Cush refers to the region South of Egypt, *i.e.* Nubia or Sudan

British scholar, T. C. Mitchell, gives these identifications for the descendents of Ham which he maintains are generally accepted.[8]

Cush	Ethiopia
Sheba	Saba (in Southern Arabia)
Dedan	Dedan (in N Arabia)
Mizraim	Egypt
Ludim	Lydia
Casluhim	Philistines
Caphtorim	Cretans
Put	Libyans
Canaan	Canaanites
Zidon	Sidon (southern Lebanon)
Heth	Hittites
Amorite	Amorites
Hivite	Hurrians
Hamathite	Hamathites

Javan is the general word for the Hellenic, or Greek, race, used throughout the Old Testament.[9]

> The territory of the Canaanite extended from Sidon
> as you go toward Gerar, as far as Gaza; as you go

---

[8] T. C. Mitchell, "Nations, Table of," New Bible Dictionary (InterVarsity Press, 1996) 904.

[9] Allen P. Ross "The Table of Nations in Genesis 10—Its Content" *Bibliotheca Sacra* 138 (1980) 22. Wenham says "Yavan" (cf. Ezek 27:13; Isa 66:19) refers in the first instance to the Ionian Greeks who lived on the coast of Turkey. But later in the OT it denotes all the Greeks, e.g., Dan 8:21; 10:20. Gordon Wenham, *Genesis*, 217. Probably the most exhaustive study of the Table is U. Cassuto, *Commentary on the Book of Genesis, Part II: From Noah to Abraham,* (Jerusalem: Magnes, 1964).

> toward Sodom and Gomorrah and Admah and
> Zeboiim, as far as Lasha. (v. 19)

Here, the Canaanites are said to range all the way from southern Lebanon down the eastern coast of the Mediterranean to Gaza. The Philistines, who later occupied Gaza, were from a different ethnic line. These Canaanites are Israel's future enemies, and this accounts for why Ham's descendents get more attention than Japheth's.

The author included no tracing of the line of Put. He puts most of the emphasis on Cush via Nimrod and Canaan

> Now Cush became the father of Nimrod; he became a mighty one on the earth. He was a mighty hunter before the Lord; therefore it is said, 'Like Nimrod a mighty hunter before the Lord.' And the beginning of his kingdom was Babel and Erech and Accad and Calneh, in the land of Shinar. From that land he went forth into Assyria, and built Nineveh and Rehoboth-Ir and Calah, and Resen between Nineveh and Calah; that is the great city.

Nimrod's story is expanded in Chapter 11, so we will deal with him there. His name means "We shall rebel."[10]

Shem

Shem gave birth to a collection of peoples called "Shemites." That was later abbreviated to "Semites."

> Sons were also born to Shem, the older brother of Japheth. Shem was the ancestor of all the descendants of Eber... (v. 11:21)

Eber is related to the word "Hebrew," so that Eber is understood to be the ancestor of the Hebrew people.[11] The

---

[10] Parunak observes: "Why is he said to rebel? Answer: civil government is one of the two forces that have always been opposed to God; the other being organized religion. People are not content to live directly under God's rule, but insist on setting themselves up over one another." cited in Paul Apple. *Commentary on Genesis*, (https://www.bibleoutlines.com/genesis-summary, 2018) 153.

[11] R. Kent Hughes, *Genesis*, 158.

line of Shem is not godly at all. They seem to stay relatively close to the fertile crescent.

The big picture

Moses gives ten generations from Adam's son Seth to Noah. Now he gives ten generations from Noah's son Shem to Abraham. That's probably not a coincidence, as argued earlier. Interestingly, we don't see the refrain "and he died" in this genealogy. It seems like death is not reigning here like it did with the others, probably because some of them were believers.

Adding the years we have available for Shem's lineage between the flood and the Tower of Babel, it could have been as little as 290 years. If so, things went down rapidly—the earlier believers not winning their own children to faith.

That's something we see today as well. Under these conditions, knowledge of the things of God literally disappears. But the disappearance is so gradual that nobody notices, nobody cares. Before long, the descendents of Noah, a righteous man, can think of nothing better to do than build the tower of Babel.

30 The Tower of Babel
Genesis 11

Background

> Now the whole land had one language and a common speech. As men moved eastward, they found a plain in Shinar and settled there. They said to each other, "Come, let's make bricks and bake them thoroughly." They used brick instead of stone, and tar for mortar. Then they said, "Come, let us build ourselves a city, with a tower that reaches to the heavens, so that we may make a name for ourselves and not be scattered over the face of the whole earth." (Genesis 11:1-4)

One language?

This story isn't claiming that there was only one language on earth. Rather, one language was in use in this "land," [*eretz*, again] i.e. the land in question—the land of Shinar, or Babylonia. Remember, *eretz* is usually translated "land" not "earth."

The previous chapter already made it plain that many languages existed (10:4 the nations were separated into their lands, every one according to his language, according to their families, into their nations). So frame of reference is important here, as always.

Was it all people on earth? Or all people in the area around Babylon? It would be a significant problem if this is a story explaining why people have different languages (like they taught in my early Sunday school). We know world languages did not come into existence at the same time. They developed in widely different times in different places. This story is not denying any of that. Interpreters should always guard against making scripture say something it doesn't really say.

If only one language existed at this point, then this chapter precedes chapter 10—a pattern unknown in Genesis. So, although some commentators think it is out of order, I'm not convinced. If this story is teaching on why people have different languages, why would confusing the tongues in Babylon make people in distant lands like Europe go to different languages? To see this as a universal event, one would have to believe that all humans were in or near Babylon at the time of this story. That's possible, but not necessary or likely.

Some argue that this is the event mentioned in the days of Peleg (10:25) when "the earth" [or land] was divided." Again, that's possible, but it suggests that humans stuck with one language for a very long time—something not backed up by archeology. Just in this region archeologists have found Akkadian, Eblaite, Elamite, Hattic, Hittite, Hurrian, Luwian, Sumerian, Urartian, and Old Persian. Certainly, the fertile crescent may have had a common trade language [Akkadian?] in addition to local languages.[1]

Their goal

Their goal was to build a city, and "a tower that reaches to the heavens." NASB says "a tower that reaches Heaven," so does the KJV. I remember even as a child thinking how preposterous it was to think they could get to heaven by building a tower! It made the story sound mythopoeic—like "Jack and the beanstalk."

Actually, the story is not far-fetched at all. They were building the city of Babylon, well known to history and the Old Testament. In it, they were planning to build a great temple. The Babylonians built "ziggurats"—large spiral or

---

[1] Akkadian, an east Semitic language, was the earliest language we know of spoken in Babylon, and it was a trade language at nearby Sumer, where they had their own language, Sumerian. This is at the dawn of writing in the early third millennium BC. Spoken language went back further into the past.

multilevel pyramids used for rituals and observing the night sky, which they believed told the future. The expression "reaches to the heavens" (a word used for the sky) means they wanted to be high up for viewing the stars.

Temples and idols

They also believed that the gods could make contact on top of the ziggurat, and that the temple was the center of the world. So, there is a sense in which they were building their way up to God, but not in some crazy, non-historical way. Like every religion apart from the gospel, they thought their works would bring them closer to God.

People the world over and throughout history build temples or shrines and view them as holy. This is universal religious behavior. An early critic of this practice was Stephen, who explains his insights during his trial in Acts 7. His whole argument centered on showing that God works in profane areas just as much as in so-called holy space—an important point for the early church, which was getting ready to leave the holy city and temple behind.

Two of Stephen's key statements bear on the tower of Babel. The first is about the Israelites when they made a golden calf,

> That was the time they made an idol in the form of a calf. They brought sacrifices to it and held a celebration in honor of *what their hands had made.* (Acts 7:41 emphasis added)

They probably got the calf idea from Egypt, but could have used many other Egyptian beast gods. The point was that their hands had made it. The fruit of our hands—that which our hands built—could easily become an idol. My company, my practice, my works of art, my house—any of these and many others are typical modern idols.

Stephen was suggesting that the Jews in his day, who virtually worshiped the temple, were repeating history.

He also reminded them of what God said to Isaiah:

However, the Most High does not live in houses made by men. As the prophet says: "Heaven is my throne, and the earth is my footstool. What kind of house will you build for me?" says the Lord. "Or where will my resting place be? Has not my hand made all these things?" (vs. 48-50, referring to Isaiah 66:1-2)

Yes! Isn't it absurd to think God needs a place to live? A place we build for him? God first pointed this out to David in 2 Samuel 7:5, "Will you build a house for me to live in?" That thought refutes itself the minute you hear it.

Israel would later have a temple approved by God, but it's important to see the difference. When Solomon opened the temple, he acknowledged,

> But will God indeed dwell on the earth? Behold, heaven and the highest heaven cannot contain You, how much less this house which I have built!
> (1 Kings 8:27)

The Old Testament temple was for teaching. The rituals carried out there were "types" or symbols, later fulfilled by Jesus and his followers, the body of Christ.

For a good and hilarious reflection on worshipping the works of our hands, see Isaiah 44:13-18, where the foolish man cuts a tree down. With half of it he cooks his dinner, with the other half he fashions an idol and bows down to it. When you think about it, worshipping the works of your hands is a way of worshipping yourself.

Underlying reasons

Their other stated goals for building the tower were to "make a name" for themselves, and that they would "not be scattered over the face of the whole earth." These in fact are the real, underlying goals.

Making a name is related to the idea of identity. To be someone, to matter, to have importance, is to make a name. In this case, the grandeur of their city and temple would set them apart from others. This is no different than what people do today, building skyscrapers, building companies, getting advanced degrees, amassing fortunes, or even preaching, all too often to prove they are important.

The inability to draw one's sense of identity from God results in an internal psychological need to establish identity through other means.

Humble people don't have this problem. They welcome anonymity and aren't worried about it at all. They know they have a name with Jesus, who "calls each of his sheep by name." They know the only name that counts is that which God gives, as when he said to Abraham, "I will... make your name great" (12:2).

But as we'll see, while Abraham's name is great, and today half the world see him as their spiritual watershed, during his lifetime almost nobody knew who he was.

How to establish one's identity is one of the great themes in scripture.

Their other goal, "Not being scattered" grows from a related fear—how will they establish their identity through their awesome city if they get scattered? So the building project was both an identity establishing project and a draw for a synthetic unity.

When people decide on self-made identity and unity, they develop God-proof systems that become a major menace.

God's response

> But the Lord came down to look at the city and the tower the people were building. "Look!" he said. "The people are united, and they all speak the same language. After this, nothing they set out to do will be impossible for them! Come, let's go down and confuse the people with different languages. Then they won't be able to understand each other." (vs. 5-7 NLT)

The account uses "anthropomorphism"—making God seem like a human. This is for our benefit. Readers trying to understand God need a bridge from our limited natures to his. It's an act of condescension on God's part to be described this way.

At the same time, God does relate to himselves, as Jesus implied when he prayed to God the Father about, "the glory which I had with You before the world was" (John 17:5). So if the persons of the godhead relate to each other, talking to each other is not farfetched, even though he probably communicates in a more elevated way than we see here. This is one of the divine dramas staged for our benefit like others in the Old Testament.

Here, the picture suggests that their massive tower is so puny that God, who dwells at such tremendous height has to stoop down to peer at it.[2]

God's assessment

God states that, because they are all united and all speak the same language, "nothing they set out to do will be impossible for them." Humans are capable of incredible technology and intellectual progress, as we see in the modern world.

Why has it taken so long for modernity to explode on the world? Humankind has progressed in technology more in the past five hundred years than in all history before that. In fact, even two hundred years ago people were plowing their fields with oxen and crossing oceans by sail—hardly different than ancient people.

The advent of modernity was a confluence of a number of key factors, but one of the biggest was the issue discussed in this passage—all being together and of one language. Throughout history, a key barrier to progress has been war. Just when a local culture is making progress, another

---

[2] R. Kent Hughes, *Genesis*, 172.

aggressive, warlike people rush in to destroy everything. This has happened all over the world again and again. People also waste their time and effort training for, manufacturing, and fighting wars.

Another problem has been people's inability to understand or appreciate each other. Language and geographical barriers kept neighboring peoples operating separately, which slowed or arrested progress.

For instance, the Chinese developed gun powder expertise very early. Meanwhile, Europe was further ahead on metallurgy. When these technologies met, after Marco Polo's journey to China, the result was firearms—and in a very short time. The opening of communication between these two cultures enabled them to use each other's discoveries, catapulting technology forward.

Today, this happens all the time. In a way never seen before, every scientific finding travels around the world through scientific journals online. Language is no barrier. Neither is geography. Instant access to research has launched science into light speed progress.

Not only knowledge and ideas, but products and services circle the earth with incredible speed and efficiency. One result is rapid progress.

This is exactly what God said would happen if humans were united and without any language barriers. "Behold, they are one people, and they all have the same language... now nothing which they purpose to do will be impossible for them" (v. 6, note the use of hyperbole).

God nullifies the project

God didn't approve of the project.

> "Come, let Us go down and there confuse their language, so that they will not understand one another's speech." So the Lord scattered them abroad from there over the face of the whole earth [or land]; and they stopped building the city. Therefore

> its name was called Babel, because there the Lord confused the language of the whole earth; and from there the Lord scattered them abroad over the face of the whole earth. (vs. 7-9)

Any time fallen humanity closes ranks and gains unification apart from God, the situation is going to deteriorate. These systems in turn compete with each other, leading to war. They protect themselves from those within who resist, leading to oppression.

This situation was headed downward. At the helm of the burgeoning metropolis was Nimrod, the mighty hunter. He stands for man's dream of empire—not just being a king, but being a king of kings.

God was not amused. At the same time he was launching his quiet plan for rescue, he found it necessary to retard humans' autonomous efforts to establish a name.

An element of satire is evident here: They named their city "Babel" (later Babylon) meaning "gateway to the gods," but God announces its real name is *"babal,"* Hebrew for confusion. It's hilarious, and a good example of God's sense of humor.

Babylon in typology

Babylon doesn't disappear after this scattering. Rather, it becomes typical of mankind's system designed to control and dominate others and glorify self apart from God. Hundreds of years later, the evil emperor Nebuchadnezzar wasted Judea after the northern kingdom of Israel had already been swept away by the Assyrians.

While in Babylon Daniel wrote his book of prophecy, including prophecy that confronted Nebuchadnezzar's determination to not only be autonomous from God but to replace God with himself.

At one point Nebuchadnezzar had a prophetic dream that revealed he was nothing but a data point on the progression of empires rising and falling as later empires destroyed the former ones. But the sequence culminated in the real empire—the kingdom of Christ (Daniel 2:35; 44-45).

Nebuchadnezzar responded by making a golden statue of himself, to signify that he was the total, all-embracing empire. Then he commanded everyone to bow before it (Daniel 3). God had to refute him through the miracle of Shadrach, Meshach, and Abed-nego in the fiery furnace.

Nebuchadnezzar is a perfect example of the Nimrod point of view when he boasts, "Is not this great Babylon, which I have built by my mighty power as a royal residence and for the glory of my majesty?" (Daniel 4:30). Then, again, God acted, smiting Nebuchadnezzar with madness until he repented.

So Babylon becomes typical of humans, unified on the basis of animism, ultimately self-worship, delighting in empire, dominating other humans, advanced human achievement, and God-proof.

The Kosmos

In the New Testament, the Babylon ideal is called the *kosmos*, or the world-system. It's nothing less than the kingdom of Satan. He lets people think they are the stars of the show, but they are all being manipulated

Jesus explained what's going on to Paul:

> I have appeared to you, to appoint you a minister and a witness... to open people's eyes so that they may turn from darkness to light and from the dominion of Satan to God, that they may receive forgiveness of sins and an inheritance among those who have been set apart by faith in Me.' (Acts 26:16-18)

In the last days, Babylon is front and center. In Revelation 17, she is "Mystery Babylon" pictured as a woman called "the great prostitute, who rules over many waters" (v. 1). Her description follows:

> A mysterious name was written on her forehead: "Babylon the Great, Mother of All Prostitutes and Obscenities in the World." I could see that she was drunk—drunk with the blood of God's holy people who were witnesses for Jesus. (vs. 5-6)

Just as humanity reaches the zenith of self-glorification and prideful unity under the beast, one voice will dissent—followers of Jesus. That won't sit well with rulers in the end times, with their zeal for godless unification. That's when the beast will finally complete the dream of Nimrod—total empire.

> They worshiped the dragon for giving the beast such power, and they also worshiped the beast. "Who is as great as the beast?" they exclaimed. "Who is able to fight against him?" ...all who dwell on the earth will worship him (Revelation 13:4, 8)

But just when it seems like human empire has expanded to the ultimate—worldwide dominion—a powerful angel descends crying, "Fallen, fallen is Babylon the great!" (Revelation 18:2).

The big picture

Babylon stands for the dream of human empire. But instead of being the gateway to the gods, it became confusion and chaos. Concerning the builders of the tower, we finally read, "And from there the Lord dispersed them over the face of all the earth [or land]" (v. 9). The thing they feared the most had come to pass.

Man's determination to exalt self flies in the face of God's will. By confusing humans' languages, God bought time to carry out his plan. Later, humans will become united again under Satan's agent—the beast. But Jesus will ride back to take over and put the world back in God's hands again. Isaiah describes Babylon's fate: "And Babylon, the glory of kingdoms, the splendor and pomp of the Chaldeans, will be

like Sodom and Gomorrah when God overthrew them"
(Isaiah 13:19).

Instead of the Babylonian ideal, God will establish final
unity in the New Jerusalem. There, the tree of life will be
"for the healing of the nations" (Revelation 22:2). Instead of
building their own empires, "The nations will walk by its
light, and the kings of the earth will bring their glory into it"
(v. 21:26).

31 Falling Ages

Throughout primordial history, the text unapologetically portrays humans living to great ages. Methuselah is the oldest. But others also live to nine hundred years. What are we to think of these claims?

First, we can be glad that the old ages in the Bible are nothing compared to the claims found in other ancient texts.

For instance, Jainism claims extreme lifespans to the Tirthankaras (their originators). Shantinatha was said to have lived for over 800,000 years before his ascension.[1] Antediluvian kings in the Sumerian King List all reign for over twenty thousand years.[2] The ages in Genesis are large, but nothing like these.

We should also consider that some animals even today live to great ages. Tortoises on the Galapagos Islands live up to several hundred years. We also know that humans will live to a thousand years in the future. God promises through Isaiah, "No more shall an infant from there live but a few days, nor an old man has not fulfilled his days; for the child shall die one hundred years old, but the sinner being one hundred years shall be accursed (Isaiah 65:20). Notice these are mortal people because they still die.[3]

As you can see from the graph, people's ages fell off rapidly after the flood. Then, some of the patriarchs made it to great age:

---

[1] http://jainmuseum.com/history-of-shantinath-bhagwan.htm.

[2] The Sumerian king list: translation, 1-39, https://web.archive.org/web/20080508061030/http:// etcsl.orinst.ox.ac.uk/section2/tr211.htm.

[3] Even secular scientists believe that things like gene sequencing might extend life to a thousand years, maybe before long. See Katie Scott, "The first person to live for 1,000 years is probably already alive" *Wired*, 13 Oct 2011.

Abraham lived 175 years (Genesis 25:7)

Isaac lived 180 years (Genesis 35:28)

Jacob lived 147 years (Genesis 47:28)

Joseph 110 years (Genesis 50:26)

Moses lived 120 years (Deuteronomy 34:7)

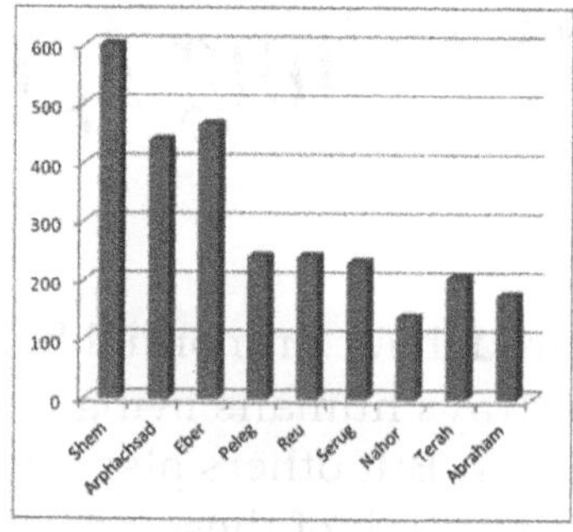

These aren't typical of life expectancies in their days. These are remarkably old men, considered to be blessed with a long life (Genesis 25:7-28). After Moses we don't find anyone older than today's ages.

Why did humans lose the ability to live to such great ages as we see in the opening chapters of Genesis?

Some commentators see this loss of longevity as a fulfillment of the judgment given in Genesis 6:3 where God said, "My Spirit shall not strive with man forever, because he also is flesh; nevertheless his days shall be one hundred and twenty years." Under this reading, God is warning that he is going to shorten the lifespan of humans, probably as an act of general judgment for sin.

I think Genesis 6:3 is referring to the length of time before the flood. The flood was definitely an act of judgment and it must have happened around one hundred and twenty years after this pronouncement. We know Noah was six hundred years old when he entered the ark (Genesis 7:6).

Although we can't show exactly how long it was between the day God made the decree and the beginning of the flood, this length of time is plausible.[4]

---

[4] If you want a mental workout, read these verses, and sort out the chronology for the ark and Noah's sons and grandsons. Genesis 6:3; 5:32; 10:21; 11:10; 9:24; 7:13; 6:18. Does this last passage mean that all Noah's sons and their wives were married before the ark began construction? Or is it predictive, and they were married by the time it sailed? And don't forget Genesis 7:6.

If this view is right, we need to look elsewhere for an explanation of the drop in ages after the flood—probably something natural.

Natural causes

One possibility is in-breeding. The flood left a single extended family alive. They generated the rest of humanity, as we saw in Chapter 10. So this was a major case of in-breeding.

In-breeding is illegal today (and throughout much of history) because of the genetic problems it causes. Recessive and often harmful genes become the norm in the inbred community. That could be the case here. Things we now consider normal maybe were not there before the flood.

Nobody knows exactly why aging happens, or why it's different for some than others. This field of study (gerontology) is pointing the finger at a number of factors in aging.

Telomeres lie at the end of chromosomes, and correct for any error in replication. Telomere shortening is associated with aging, mortality and aging-related diseases. So this could have changed around the time of the flood.

A number of key hormones and enzymes that play important roles in cell proliferation, DNA checking, and other functions are typically deficient in elderly people. The result is declining tissue health. Science is unclear on why these changes happen, and whether they could be prevented.

Humans are different than many mammals and most other animals, because we live long past our time of fertility. This points to special creation of humans rather than Darwinian adaptation which would normally select against such waste.

Genes associated with aging and lifespan have been affected as a result of the Fall, either directly through mutations, or indirectly through genetic bottlenecks.

We should be able to live longer, because we are constantly changing out old tissue with new. Our skin, for example, never gets older than one month. New cells are continually produced (by cell division) deep in the epidermis, while the older ones continually slough off at the surface.

Similarly, the cells lining our intestines completely replace themselves every five to seven days; our red blood cells are entirely replaced about every ninety days; and our white blood cells are replaced about every week.

Scientists believe that little or nothing in our body is more than about 10 years old at the molecular level. Thus, thanks to cell turnover and replacement, most of the organs in the body of a 90-year-old man are perhaps no older than those of a child. And yet, cell reproduction fails to maintain the quality in tissues we had when young.

So there is no clear reason why people couldn't live much longer than we do today.

The big picture

Patriarchal history begins in verse 27 with *toledot* six: "Now these are the generations of Terah."

The story goes forward in Volume II. We haven't divided the discussion here because Genesis 12 and following is different history than Genesis 1-11. They are the same. Our reason for dividing our coverage into two volumes is that readers today are intimidated by six hundred page books. They also cost too much.

Genesis, the gateway into the Bible, isn't finished. We invite you to continue reading as God refines his plan while laying down some of the most important theological markers and themes that govern the rest of scripture.